INDIANA SOCIAL Studies

Indiana History

Reading Support and Intervention

D1385271

HOUGHTON MIFFLIN HARCOURT
School Publishers

ISBN-13: 978-0-15-377079-1
ISBN-10: 0-15-377079-1

2 3 4 5 6 7 8 9 10 0982 17 16 15 14 13 12 11 10 09

Contents

Unit 4

Introduction

Today's students are growing up in the Information Age. Our concept of literacy is expanding and changing. In our technological society, students need to understand and evaluate information in many forms—websites, e-mail, Internet advertisements, trade books, newspapers, and magazines—in addition to their textbooks.

WHY is it important to offer reading support to students in the context of social studies instruction? To succeed in social studies, students must be able to read and make meaning from expository text. The structure of social studies text is very different from the more familiar structure of stories and fiction selections. The organizational pattern of social studies text is likely to be different from texts in other content areas.

Students come to us with varying levels of English proficiency and literacy, as well as a variety of backgrounds and experiences. As we assess and plan for the individual needs of our students in grades 3–6, we identify students who are struggling to comprehend grade-level expository texts. This puts them at a disadvantage. In order for students to learn about the world, past and present, they must be able to connect ideas within a text and also to connect prior knowledge to ideas in a text.

Research shows that we can help students better understand and remember what they read by

- using **direct vocabulary instruction** to teach words that are important to concepts in their reading.
- providing **systematic fluency practice**, through rereadings and feedback, to help students improve their fluency.
- teaching students how and when to **use comprehension strategies** to understand expository text.

HOW can we effectively offer reading support to students in the context of social studies instruction? Teachers need an organized, systematic way to help struggling students access on-grade level texts and materials. *Reading Support and Intervention* gives social studies teachers a practical guide for helping these students. Materials include

- A guide that supplements the *Indiana Social Studies Teacher Edition* with clear and specific suggestions for supporting struggling readers throughout each lesson.
- Student pages that provide vocabulary and concept words, as well as fluency practice, for each lesson. Graphic organizers are also provided to help students focus on important concepts and monitor their comprehension.
- Procedure Cards for teaching vocabulary, fluency, previewing, and comprehension of expository text.
- Student Cards to guide students in using helpful strategies as they read their social studies text in cooperative learning groups.
- Word Cards that represent the vocabulary words taught in the *Indiana Social Studies Student Edition*, along with their glossary definitions.

Using *Reading Support and Intervention*

Each lesson in *Reading Support and Intervention* corresponds to lessons in the *Indiana Social Studies Teacher Edition.* The instructional model presented in this book is best suited for small groups of students who need direct and explicit reading instruction at different times during the social studies lesson. The information presented below will show how to use *Reading Support and Intervention* in conjunction with *Harcourt Social Studies* lessons.

BEFORE . . . starting a new lesson in *Indiana Social Studies*

Teach Vocabulary Strategies
- *Reading Support and Intervention* lesson
- Procedure Card 1
- *Reading Support and Intervention* student vocabulary/fluency page
- Word Cards

Help Build Fluency
- *Reading Support and Intervention* lesson
- Procedure Card 2
- *Reading Support and Intervention* student vocabulary/fluency page

DURING . . . the lesson in *Indiana Social Studies*

Support Text Comprehension
- *Reading Support and Intervention* Preview the Lesson
- Procedure Card 3
- *Reading Support and Intervention* Build Comprehension of Expository Text
- *Reading Support and Intervention* student comprehension page
- Procedure Card 4
- Student Cards 1–3

AFTER . . . the lesson in *Indiana Social Studies*

Facilitate Responses to Expository Text
- *Reading Support and Intervention* student comprehension page
- *Reading Support and Intervention* Summarize/Review and Respond
- Leveled Readers
- Procedure Card 5
- Student Cards 1–3

Teaching Vocabulary

WHAT does research tell us about the importance of direct vocabulary instruction?
As students read expository texts, they are sure to encounter words whose meanings they do not know. Such words may represent key social studies concepts that students are unfamiliar with. Students will not be able to comprehend the text without knowing what the words mean.

Research has shown that the direct teaching of specific words before reading will result in improved reading comprehension. The vocabulary words identified in each *Indiana Social Studies* lesson are included on the student vocabulary/fluency pages in *Reading Support and Intervention*. Students practice reading aloud vocabulary words along with additional concept words that should be helpful to struggling readers. The program introduces Additional Words that appear in the lesson and that are important to understanding key concepts. Some of these words may be unfamiliar to students who are reading below grade level. Others may be words introduced in earlier lessons in *Indiana Social Studies* that are also important in the upcoming lesson. Reviewing the meanings of the words and reading them in text-related sentences will help students read the lesson and understand it better.

Word Cards are provided in *Reading Support and Intervention* to aid in direct vocabulary instruction.

Teaching Fluency

WHY do we need to teach fluency in the context of social studies instruction? Fluency is the ability to read a text quickly and with accuracy. Fluent readers recognize words in print and group the words into chunks, such as phrases and clauses. As a result, these students can focus their attention on making connections between concepts and on understanding what they read. By helping less-fluent readers improve their fluency, we help them become better social studies learners.

HOW can we teach fluency? Research tells us that repeated oral readings of a text, with the teacher providing guidance or feedback, helps students improve their fluency and their comprehension. *Reading Support and Intervention* provides sentences with Vocabulary and Additional Words in context, as well as suggestions for fluency practice. The teacher models fluent reading and guides students in oral rereadings.

Previewing the Lesson

HOW can previewing the lesson help struggling readers better understand the text?
Research tells us that good readers intuitively set a purpose for reading.
Previewing a lesson helps students become familiar with the text so that they
can set a purpose for reading it. After previewing, they read to learn about the
topics they have previewed, to find out specific information about those topics,
and to answer specific questions.

We also know that students learn by connecting new information to information
they already know. Previewing activates students' prior knowledge about
concepts they will encounter in the lesson. The preview helps them understand
the chronology of historic events and helps them see how these events are
related to other events that preceded and followed them.

Building Comprehension of Expository Text

WHAT strategies can students use to increase their understanding of expository text?
Research has identified specific strategies that students can use to improve their
reading comprehension. Strategies emphasized in *Reading Support and Intervention*
include

- monitoring comprehension.
- using graphic organizers.
- answering questions.

HOW can we help students monitor their comprehension? Students who monitor their
understanding as they read are better able to master social studies content. In order
to monitor their comprehension, students must learn to think metacognitively.
That is, they must learn to think about their thinking. As they read, good readers
assess whether or not they understand the content. They choose and use
appropriate strategies, such as rereading portions of the text, adjusting their
reading rate according to the difficulty of the material, restating passages in their
own words, and pausing occasionally to summarize what they have just read.

The Preview the Lesson and the Build Comprehension of Expository Text sections
in *Reading Support and Intervention* provide opportunities for you to teach strategies
for monitoring comprehension. As you guide students through the lesson and
observe where they have problems, you can suggest appropriate strategies to help
resolve the difficulty. Explain how the strategy can help them and when to apply it.

Students can also use the KWL, SQ3R or QAR strategy to help them monitor
their comprehension as they read. Student Cards are available that provide
guidance in using these strategies.

Summarizing the Lesson

WHY is using graphic organizers an important strategy for social studies? Graphic organizers include webs, charts, graphs, and diagrams. The purpose of a graphic organizer is to show how concepts are related. Graphic organizers such as time lines and flowcharts show how events are related chronologically. Other types of graphic organizers show cause-and-effect relationships, comparisons and contrasts between concepts, or how details relate to a main idea.

Completing the *Reading Support and Intervention* graphic organizer for each lesson helps students focus on important concepts in the lesson. Filling in the organizer as they read also helps them monitor their comprehension of the material. The completed organizer gives them a tool that they can use to recall relationships in the text and to summarize what they read.

WHAT does research tell us about the value of answering questions? Having students answer questions about their reading is a traditional strategy that teachers have used to guide and assess learning. Recent research confirms the value of this strategy. Answering questions improves students' comprehension of social studies concepts by

- giving them a purpose for reading the text.
- focusing their attention on the content.
- encouraging them to monitor their comprehension and think metacognitively.
- helping them review what they have learned and relate it to other knowledge.

Support metacognitive thinking and strategy use by asking students to explain how they figured out correct answers or how they can find answers that they do not know.

HOW can Leveled Readers help struggling readers? The Leveled Readers were specifically produced to match the content of *Indiana Social Studies*. The readers are categorized into three reading levels: Basic, Proficient, and Advanced. These readers can help build fluency when used for small-group reading, shared reading, echo reading, choral reading, or reading at home.

LESSON 1 # The Geography of Indiana

Vocabulary Strategies

Preteach Additional Vocabulary After teaching the Vocabulary words on Student Edition page 12, explain to students that there are several other important words they will see in this lesson. Use Procedure Card 1, along with the suggestions below, to introduce the words.

geographic	Point out the root *geo*, meaning "Earth." Related words include *geography* and *geographer*.
landform	Have students give examples of landforms, such as mountains, hills, and deserts.
ridge	Ask a volunteer to draw a chain of hills. Explain that a long chain of hills is called a ridge.
waterfall	Have students identify the two shorter words that make up this compound word. Point out the photograph of a waterfall on page 14.
hub	Draw a wheel and point out the hub. Then have students read and discuss this sentence: "Evansville is an important hub, or center of activity, for the area where Indiana, Illinois, and Kentucky meet."

WORD CARDS To help teach the lesson vocabulary, use the Word Cards on pages 121–122.

Build Fluency

Use page 4 and the steps on Procedure Card 2 to reinforce vocabulary and build fluency. Read each vocabulary word aloud and have students repeat it. Then have students work in pairs to reread the words. Follow a similar procedure with the phrases and sentences. Continue to help students build fluency by having them reread "You Are There" in the Student Edition.

Text Comprehension

BEFORE READING

Preview the Lesson Guide students in previewing the lesson using Procedure Card 3. Point out the following features of the lesson on Student Edition pages 12–17.

• **Pages 12–13** Read the lesson title and discuss the "What to Know" question. Explain that there are different ways to describe where a place is located. Invite students to suggest possible answers. Preview the illustration that shows Indiana's location, and have students answer the question in the caption.

• **Pages 14–15** Preview the photograph of a waterfall on page 14 and the map of Indiana's Land and Water on page 15. Discuss the map skill question.

• **Pages 16–17** Have students examine the population table, the photograph of Lafayette on pages 16–17, and the photograph of Evansville on page 17. Have students answer the question in the caption about the populations of these two cities. Then preview the Review questions on page 17.

DURING READING

Build Comprehension of Expository Text Present the graphic organizer on page 5. Have students preview the organizer by filling in the lesson title and comparing the three main heads in the organizer with the matching subheads in the Student Edition pages 12–17. Tell students that the section subheads provide additional help with identifying important information. Use Procedure Card 4, the Reading Check questions in *Indiana Social Studies*, and the directed reading suggestions below.

- **Page 12** After students have read "You Are There," discuss how they might answer the pen pal's questions.

- **Page 13** Have students read "Indiana in the United States" and discuss different ways of describing Indiana's location. Then have them examine the first box in the organizer. Point out the subheads "A Midwestern State" and "Relative Location" that match the section subheads in the text. Help students locate information under each of those section subheads to fill in the blanks.

- **Pages 14–15** After students have read "Indiana's Land and Water," have them fill in the next box of the organizer, using the three subheads to help them locate information in the text. For "Plains and Hills," tell students to give brief descriptions of the land in each part of the state.

- **Pages 16–17** Have students read "Indiana's Cities" and complete the organizer. For the first subhead, "The State Capital," students should write the name of the capital and its location in the state. Then they can list other cities in the same part of the state. For the other subheads, have students list major cities in northern Indiana and southern Indiana.

AFTER READING

Summarize Have students use their completed graphic organizers to summarize the lesson. Then have them compare their summaries to the lesson summary on page 17.

Review and Respond Work through the Review questions with students. Use Focus Skill Transparency 1, Main Idea and Details, to discuss main ideas and supporting details mentioned in the lesson.

Make a Book Cover Have students recall what an atlas is. You may want to provide one or more examples of atlases. Suggest that students reread passages in their text and list physical and human features they would like to show on the maps they will create for their book covers.

Leveled Readers Use the Leveled Readers and Procedure Card 5 to build fluency and comprehension.

Name _____   Date _____

DIRECTIONS Read aloud the words in Part A. Practice reading aloud the phrases and the sentences in Part B.

Part A

Vocabulary Words		Additional Words
region	fertile soil	geographic
relative location	tributary	landform
border	human feature	ridge
physical feature	industry	waterfall
plain		hub

Part B

1. Indiana / is in the Midwest, / one of the five geographic regions / of the United States.

2. You can describe / Indiana's relative location / by naming the four other states / that share its borders.

3. Indiana's physical features / include its landforms / and bodies of water.

4. The fertile soils / of Indiana's plains / support much of the state's farming.

5. The hills of southern Indiana / include features such as waterfalls, / caves, / and ridges.

6. Along its route, / the Wabash River / is joined by several tributaries.

7. Some lakes in central and southern Indiana / are human features.

8. Fort Wayne / has a growing health-care industry.

9. Evansville / is an important hub / for the area where Indiana, / Illinois, / and Kentucky / meet.

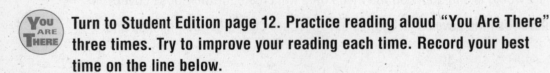 Turn to Student Edition page 12. Practice reading aloud "You Are There" three times. Try to improve your reading each time. Record your best time on the line below.

Number of words ___82___   My Best Time _____   Words per Minute _____

Name _____ Date _____

Lesson Title: _____

Indiana in the United States

A Midwestern State

Region Indiana is in _____

Relative Location

Shares borders with _____ other states

Indiana's Land and Water

Plains and Hills

Northern two-thirds of Indiana _____

Southern one-third of Indiana _____

Rivers   Indiana's longest river _____

Lakes   Where many lakes are found _____

Indiana's Cities

The State Capital _____ Location _____

Other cities _____

Cities in Northern Indiana _____

Cities in Southern Indiana _____

LESSON 2 ## Physical Regions of Indiana

Vocabulary Strategies

Preteach Additional Vocabulary After teaching the Vocabulary words on Student Edition page 20, explain to students that there are several other important words they will see in this lesson. Use Procedure Card 1, along with the suggestions below, to introduce the words.

landscape	Point out the shorter word *land* that is part of this word. Explain that the photographs on pages 20–21, 23, and 25 show different types of landscapes.
deposit	Discuss meanings students may know, such as making a bank deposit. Then discuss this context: "(Glaciers) ... created underground deposits of water and minerals."
valley	Ask a volunteer to draw a sketch of two hills and point out the valley between them.
strip	Have students cut scrap paper into strips. Then ask students to describe a strip of land.
westernmost	Have students identify the word *west* and suffixes *-ern* and *-most*. Point out three states or cities on a map, and challenge students to identify the westernmost one.

WORD CARDS To help teach the lesson vocabulary, use the Word Cards on pages 121–124.

Build Fluency

Use page 8 and the steps on Procedure Card 2 to reinforce vocabulary and build fluency. Read each vocabulary word aloud and have students repeat it. Then have students work in pairs to reread the words. Follow a similar procedure with the phrases and sentences. Continue to help students build fluency by having them reread "You Are There" in the Student Edition.

Text Comprehension

BEFORE READING

Preview the Lesson Guide students in previewing the lesson using Procedure Card 3. Point out the following features of the lesson on Student Edition pages 20–25.

• **Pages 20–21** Paraphrase the "What to Know" question: *What is special or different about each of Indiana's physical regions?* Preview the photograph of a present-day glacier and the small inset map of glaciers of the Ice Age. Explain that the land of Indiana was shaped long ago by the glaciers shown on the map. Have students read and discuss the Fast Fact.

• **Pages 22–23** Preview the map of Indiana's three physical regions, and have students answer the map skill question. Preview the photographs of Indiana Dunes National Lakeshore and farmland in the Central Till Plain on page 23. Have students locate these places on the map on page 22.

- **Pages 24–25** Have students read the Children in History feature about the Hiestand children and the discovery of Marengo Cave. Discuss the Make it Relevant question. Preview the photograph of sinkholes on page 25, and have students locate the Southern Hills and Lowlands region on the map on page 22. Then preview the Review questions on page 25.

DURING READING

Build Comprehension of Expository Text Present the graphic organizer on page 9. Have students preview the organizer by filling in the lesson title and comparing the four main heads in the organizer with the matching subheads in the Student Edition pages 20–25. Tell students that the section subheads provide additional help with identifying important information. Use Procedure Card 4, the Reading Check questions in *Indiana Social Studies*, and the directed reading suggestions below.

- **Page 20** After students have read "You Are There," have them trace the family's route on the map on page 22. Ask students to show where the land is mostly hilly and where it becomes flat.

- **Page 21** Have students read "Rivers of Ice" and identify the major force that shaped Indiana's land. In the first box of the organizer, point out the two subheads that match the section subheads in the text. Guide students in completing the box.

- **Page 22** After students have read "Northern Moraine and Lake," guide them in filling in the next box of the organizer.

- **Page 23** Have students read "Central Till Plain" and fill in the next box in the organizer. Point out that the information about the location of the Central Till Plain can be found in the section of the text before the section subhead "Flat, Fertile Land."

- **Pages 24–25** Now students can read "Southern Hills and Lowlands" and complete the organizer, using the subheads to locate information. Point out the arrows that connect three of the boxes, and ask what students think these arrows mean. Discuss the idea that someone traveling through Indiana from north to south would pass through the three physical regions in this order.

AFTER READING

Summarize Have students use their completed graphic organizers to summarize the lesson. Then have them compare their summaries to the lesson summary on page 25.

Review and Respond Work through the Review questions with students. If students need additional help identifying main ideas and details, use Focus Skill Transparency 1.

Write a Report Suggest that students reread and take notes on the section of the lesson that tells about their chosen region. Remind them to describe features of the region and to tell in their own words how glaciers created or affected those features.

Leveled Readers Use the Leveled Readers and Procedure Card 5 to build fluency and comprehension.

Name _____ Date _____

Read aloud the words in Part A. Practice reading aloud the phrases and the sentences in Part B.

Part A

Vocabulary Words		Additional Words	
glacier	till	landscape	westernmost
lithosphere	elevation	deposit	
wetland	canyon	valley	
dune	sinkhole	strip	

Part B

1. The glaciers of long ago / greatly affected / parts of Earth's lithosphere.

2. The landscape and environment / of Indiana today / are related to the glaciers / of the past.

3. Glaciers / created underground deposits / of water and minerals.

4. In the Northern Moraine and Lake region, / deposits of sandy soil and water / created wetlands.

5. Today, / dunes can be seen / at Indiana Dunes National Lakeshore.

6. While most of the Central Till Plain / is low, flat land, / the region / also has low, rolling hills / and small valleys.

7. Scenic canyons / lie along the Wabash River / and many of its tributaries.

8. The westernmost strip of lowland / in southern Indiana / has an elevation / of about 500 feet above sea level.

9. Sinkholes / are a main feature / of the next lowland.

You ARE THERE Turn to Student Edition page 20. Practice reading aloud "You Are There" three times. Try to improve your reading each time. Record your best time on the line below.

Number of words ___63___ My Best Time _____ Words per Minute _____

Name _____ Date _____

Lesson Title: _____

Rivers of Ice

Shaping Earth What created landforms _____

Shaping Indiana How _____

_____

_____

Northern Moraine and Lake

Lakes, Wetlands, and Dunes What this region covers _____

Eastern part _____ Western part _____

Where dunes are located _____

Central Till Plain

Where _____

Flat, Fertile Land Provides Indiana with _____

Southern Hills and Lowlands

What this region covers _____

Lowlands and Uplands Pattern _____

_____

Caves, Sinkholes, and Knobs Highest knob _____

LESSON 3 # Climate and Wildlife of Indiana

Vocabulary Strategies

Preteach Additional Vocabulary After teaching the Vocabulary words on Student Edition page 28, explain to students that there are several other important words they will see in this lesson. Use Procedure Card 1, along with the suggestions below, to introduce the words.

temperate	Write *temperate* and *temperature*, and point out the similarity between these two words. Have students use this context clue to tell the meaning of *temperate*: "A temperate climate is usually neither very hot nor very cold."
humid	Give *moist* and *damp* as synonyms for *humid*.
rotate	Tell students that this word is from the Latin *rota*, meaning "wheel." Ask them to imagine a bicycle wheel spinning around and around. The wheel is rotating. A related word is *rotation*.
hemisphere	On a globe of the world, ask students to identify the Northern, Southern, Western, and Eastern Hemispheres. Explain that *hemi* means "half" and a sphere is a shape like a ball or a globe.
cycle	Tell students that this word is from the Greek word *kyklos*, which has the same meaning as the Latin *rota*: "wheel." Call attention to the diagram of the water cycle on page 31, and discuss how the movement of the water is like a wheel.

WORD CARDS To help teach the lesson vocabulary, use the Word Cards on pages 123–124.

Build Fluency

Use page 12 and the steps on Procedure Card 2 to reinforce vocabulary and build fluency. Read each vocabulary word aloud and have students repeat it. Then have students work in pairs to reread the words. Follow a similar procedure with the phrases and sentences. Continue to help students build fluency by having them reread "You Are There" in the Student Edition.

Text Comprehension

BEFORE READING

Preview the Lesson Guide students in previewing the lesson using Procedure Card 3. Point out the following features of the lesson on Student Edition pages 28–33.

- **Pages 28–29** Read and discuss the "What to Know" question. Preview the photographs of Indiana in fall, winter, spring, and summer.

- **Pages 30–31** Have students examine the diagram of the four seasons on page 30 and discuss the question in the caption. Then preview and discuss the water cycle diagram on page 31. Have students answer the question in the caption.

- **Pages 32–33** Preview the illustration of Indiana Wildlife on page 32. Have students use the key to identify the plants and animals, and to answer the question in the caption. Preview the photograph of a chipmunk and the Review questions on page 33.

DURING READING

Build Comprehension of Expository Text Present the graphic organizer on page 13. Have students preview the organizer by filling in the lesson title and comparing the four main heads. in the organizer with the matching subheads in the Student Edition pages 28–33. Tell students that the section subheads provide additional help with identifying important information. Use Procedure Card 4, the Reading Check questions in *Indiana Social Studies*, and the directed reading suggestions below.

- **Page 28** After students have read "You Are There," ask them to name plants, animals, and birds that they may have seen in parks, near their homes, or other places in Indiana.

- **Page 29** Have students read "Indiana's Climate" and discuss the type of climate Indiana has and how the seasons vary. Then have students fill in the first box in the graphic organizer.

- **Page 30** After students have read "Earth and Sun," point out the cause and effect statements in the second box of the organizer. Tell students to write the effect for each cause. Point out that these causes and effects can be found in the text under the section subhead "The Science of Seasons."

- **Page 31** Have students read "Precipitation." Ask volunteers to explain the water cycle and the lake effect. Then have students fill in the next box in the organizer. Remind them to use the section subheads to help locate information in the text.

- **Pages 32–33** After students have read "Indiana's Wildlife," tell them to list at least four examples of plants and four examples of animals, in addition to the state tree and state bird, that they read about in this section of the lesson.

AFTER READING

Summarize Have students use their completed graphic organizers to summarize the lesson. Then have them compare their summaries to the lesson summary on page 33.

Review and Respond Work through the Review questions with students. If students need additional help identifying main ideas and details, use Focus Skill Transparency 1.

Design a Park You may want to offer students a choice of appropriate print and online sources to use for their research. Have students work in small groups to carry out their research and design a park. Discuss how they might draw a plan for their park and create a key to indicate types of plants and trees.

Leveled Readers Use the Leveled Readers and Procedure Card 5 to build fluency and comprehension.

Name _____ Date _____

DIRECTIONS Read aloud the words in Part A. Practice reading aloud the phrases and the sentences in Part B.

Part A

Vocabulary Words		Additional Words	
climate	drought	temperate	hemisphere
tornado	hydrosphere	humid	cycle
precipitation	biosphere	rotate	

Part B

1. Indiana / has a temperate climate.

2. Summer / is hot and humid / because warm air pushes up / from the Gulf of Mexico.

3. Both spring and summer / also bring tornadoes.

4. At times, / southern Indiana / has droughts, / or long periods / of little or no precipitation.

5. As Earth rotates on its axis, / it also travels around the sun.

6. When the Northern Hemisphere / is tilted toward the sun, / it is summer there.

7. Precipitation / in Indiana and other places / is part of the water cycle.

8. The water cycle / is water's movement / in the hydrosphere.

9. Indiana's biosphere / is rich / in plant and animal life.

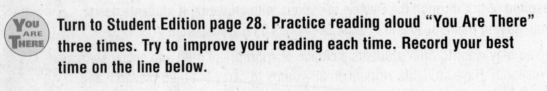 Turn to Student Edition page 28. Practice reading aloud "You Are There" three times. Try to improve your reading each time. Record your best time on the line below.

Number of words ___83___ My Best Time _____ Words per Minute _____

Name _____ Date _____

Lesson Title: _____

Indiana's Climate

Type of climate _____

Varied Seasons   What is tied to seasons

_____

_____

Earth and Sun

The Science of Seasons

CAUSE: The Northern Hemisphere is tilted towards the sun.

EFFECT: _____

CAUSE: The Northern Hemisphere is tilted away from the sun.

EFFECT: _____

Precipitation

The Lake Effect   What affects Indiana's weather

_____

Precipitation Varies   Average _____

_____

Indiana's Wildlife

Plants   State tree _____   Examples of other plants

_____

Animals   State bird _____   Examples of other animals

_____

LESSON 4 # People and Resources of Indiana

Vocabulary Strategies

Preteach Additional Vocabulary After teaching the Vocabulary words on Student Edition page 34, explain to students that there are several other important words they will see in this lesson. Use Procedure Card 1, along with the suggestions below, to introduce the words.

lumber	Explain that after trees have been cut down and sawed into pieces, the wood is called lumber.
modify	Give *change* as a synonym for *modify*. Have students read this sentence and then reread it, substituting *changed* for *modified*: "Over the past 200 years, people in Indiana have modified the landscape in many ways."
dam	Display one or more pictures of dams. Invite students to share what they know about why people build dams and what happens as a result.
replanted	Have students identify the base word *plant*, prefix *re-*, meaning "again," and ending *-ed*. Then have them read and define the word.
services	Use these context sentences to guide students in defining *services*: "The growth of cities also causes more demand for services. People need more water, electricity, schools, and trash removal."

WORD CARDS To help teach the lesson vocabulary, use the Word Cards on pages 123–126.

Build Fluency

Use page 16 and the steps on Procedure Card 2 to reinforce vocabulary and build fluency. Read each vocabulary word aloud and have students repeat it. Then have students work in pairs to reread the words. Follow a similar procedure with the phrases and sentences. Continue to help students build fluency by having them reread "You Are There" in the Student Edition.

Text Comprehension

BEFORE READING

Preview the Lesson Guide students in previewing the lesson using Procedure Card 3. Point out the following features of the lesson on Student Edition pages 34–39.

- **Pages 34–35** Read and discuss the "What to Know" question. Preview the photographs of Loblolly Marsh and of author Gene Stratton-Porter on page 34, and the photographs of farmland and limestone mining on page 35. Have students identify the product shown in the smaller image to the left of each caption on page 35.

- **Pages 36–37** Have students examine the photographs and map. After students have answered the map skill question, discuss what these photographs and this map show about ways that Hoosiers have modified Indiana's land.

- **Pages 38–39** Preview the aerial-view photograph of a suburb and the Review questions on page 38. Call attention to the biography of Gene Stratton-Porter on page 39. Have students recall what they learned about Stratton-Porter earlier in their preview.

DURING READING

Build Comprehension of Expository Text Present the graphic organizer on page 17. Have students preview the organizer by filling in the lesson title and comparing the three main heads in the organizer with the matching subheads in the Student Edition pages 34–38. Tell students that the section subheads provide additional help with identifying important information. Use Procedure Card 4, the Reading Check questions in *Indiana Social Studies*, and the directed reading suggestions below.

- **Page 34** After students have read "You Are There," have them identify the various ways that people have used and changed this wetland over the years.

- **Page 35** Have students read "Indiana's Resources." Point out the boxes in the graphic organizer with subheads that match the section subheads in the text. Tell students to list in each box the natural resources they read about in the corresponding section of the lesson.

- **Pages 36–37** After students have read "Modifying the Land," have them list in each box ways that people modified the land for that purpose. Point out that the subheads in the boxes match the four section subheads in the text.

- **Page 38** Have students read "Urban Challenges" and complete the organizer by writing an effect or effects for each cause.

AFTER READING

Summarize Have students use their completed graphic organizers to summarize the lesson. Then have them compare their summaries to the lesson summary on page 38.

Review and Respond Work through the Review questions with students. If students need additional help identifying main ideas and details, use Focus Skill Transparency 1.

Make a Map Have students look back at the map on page 37. Point out that this map shows three different kinds of transportation routes in Indiana by 1860. Discuss how the maps that students create will be different from this map. You may want to have students work in pairs or small groups.

Leveled Readers Use the Leveled Readers and Procedure Card 5 to build fluency and comprehension.

Name _____ Date _____

Read aloud the words in Part A. Practice reading aloud the phrases and the sentences in Part B.

Part A

Vocabulary Words		Additional Words	
natural resource	rural	lumber	services
agriculture	urban	modify	
mineral	suburb	dam	
canal		replanted	

Part B

1. Indiana / is rich in natural resources.

2. Fertile soil / and flat land / make much of Indiana / good for agriculture.

3. The Southern Hills and Lowlands region / has valuable deposits of minerals.

4. People use trees / from Indiana's forests / for lumber, / paper, / and other products.

5. Over the past 200 years, / people in Indiana / have modified the land / by building canals and dams, / and in many other ways.

6. Hoosiers / also replanted / many of the state's forests / that had been cleared in the 1800s.

7. Beginning in the late 1800s, / many Hoosiers / moved from rural areas / to urban areas.

8. Today, / nearly three out of every four Hoosiers / live in a city or a suburb.

9. The growth of cities / causes more demand for services.

YOU ARE THERE Turn to Student Edition page 34. Practice reading aloud "You Are There" three times. Try to improve your reading each time. Record your best time on the line below.

Number of words ___71___   My Best Time _____   Words per Minute _____

Name _____ Date _____

Lesson Title: _____

Indiana's Resources

Crop Regions
Natural Resources

From Fuels to Forests
Natural Resources

Modifying the Land

Farmland

Transportation

Fuels, Dams, and Forests

The Growth of Cities

Urban Challenges

CAUSE: More cars on the roads

EFFECTS: _____

CAUSE: More people living in cities

EFFECT: _____

LESSON 5 **People of Indiana**

Vocabulary Strategies

Preteach Additional Vocabulary After teaching the Vocabulary words on Student Edition page 44, explain to students that there are several other important words they will see in this lesson. Use Procedure Card 1, along with the suggestions below, to introduce the words.

square mile	Draw a square and have students identify the shape. Explain that a square mile of land is I mile long on each side. Have a volunteer label the sides of the square *I mile*.
festival	Ask students to name and describe briefly any festivals they may have attended. Point out and discuss festivals shown in the photographs on page 47.
reenactment	Point out prefixes *re-* and *en-*, base word *act*, and suffix *-ment*. Explain that a reenactment is an event at which people dress in historic costumes and act out scenes from history.
belief	Write *believe* and *belief.* Have students compare and discuss the meanings of the two words.

WORD CARDS To help teach the lesson vocabulary, use the Word Cards on pages 125–126.

Build Fluency

Use page 20 and the steps on Procedure Card 2 to reinforce vocabulary and build fluency. Read each vocabulary word aloud and have students repeat it. Then have students work in pairs to reread the words. Follow a similar procedure with the phrases and sentences. Continue to help students build fluency by having them reread "You Are There" in the Student Edition.

Text Comprehension

BEFORE READING

Preview the Lesson Guide students in previewing the lesson using Procedure Card 3. Point out the following features of the lesson on Student Edition pages 44–49.

- **Pages 44–45** Read aloud the "What to Know" question. Preview the photograph of students on page 44. Ask how all students in Indiana of different backgrounds and cultures are alike. (*All are Hoosiers.*) Have students examine the photograph of people at a football game in Indianapolis and the population density graph on page 45. Discuss the question in the caption. Help students understand how the density of Indiana's population can be greater than the density of the population of the entire United States, even though the population of the United States is, of course, much larger than Indiana's.

- **Pages 46–47** Point out the illustration of the mandolin on page 46. Students may notice that it looks similar to a guitar. Ask whether students have ever heard someone play a mandolin. Have students examine and discuss the map of Indiana's culture on page 47.

- **Pages 48–49** Point out and discuss the photographs of different houses of worship and worshippers on pages 48 and 49. Then preview the Review questions on page 49.

DURING READING

Build Comprehension of Expository Text Present the graphic organizer on page 21. Have students preview the organizer by filling in the lesson title and comparing the three main heads in the organizer with the matching subheads in the Student Edition pages 44–49. Tell students that the section subheads provide additional help with identifying important information. Use Procedure Card 4, the Reading Check questions in *Indiana Social Studies*, and the directed reading suggestions below.

- **Page 44** Have students read "You Are There." Invite volunteers to name items they might bring to share if you were having a World Culture Day at your school. Encourage students to explain why they would choose these items.

- **Page 45** After students have read "Indiana's Population," have them complete the first box in the organizer. Guide students in using the section subheads to find the information they need.

- **Pages 46–47** Have students read "Where Hoosiers Come From." Discuss briefly how the arrival of different groups of people has contributed to the state's diversity. Then have students fill in the corresponding box in the organizer. Point out that the first item of information can be found before the first section subhead in the text. Remind students to use the section subheads to locate information.

- **Pages 48–49** Have students read "Religion in Indiana" and complete the organizer.

AFTER READING

Summarize Have students use their completed graphic organizers to summarize the lesson. Then have them compare their summaries to the lesson summary on page 49.

Review and Respond Work through the Review questions with students. If students need additional help identifying main ideas and details, use Focus Skill Transparency 1.

Give a Speech Have students look back at their texts and list ethnic groups that have had an effect on Indiana. Then discuss how students may go about their research. You may want to provide some appropriate research materials and identify keywords for research online. After students have planned their speeches, have them practice with partners before giving their speeches to the class.

Leveled Readers Use the Leveled Readers and Procedure Card 5 to build fluency and comprehension.

Name _____ Date _____

DIRECTIONS Read aloud the words in Part A. Practice reading aloud the phrases and the sentences in Part B.

Part A

Vocabulary Words		Additional Words
culture	heritage	square mile
immigrant	ethnic group	festival
population density		reenactment
population distribution		belief

Part B

1. The average population density of Indiana / is about 170 people / per square mile.

2. Population densities vary / because of population distribution.

3. Throughout Indiana, / the population densities of the state's cities / are higher / than those of its rural areas.

4. In the early 1900s, / immigrants came / to work in the state's mills / and factories.

5. Festivals held all over Indiana / are one way people share / their heritage.

6. Many festivals / are held by ethnic groups.

7. They celebrate / the heritages / of many different cultures.

8. Indiana's museums and states parks / provide displays, / performances, / and living history reenactments.

9. Early settlers / brought Protestant beliefs / to the region.

 Turn to Student Edition page 44. Practice reading aloud "You Are There" three times. Try to improve your reading each time. Record your best time on the line below.

Number of words ___66___ My Best Time _____ Words per Minute _____

Name _____ Date _____

Lesson Title: _____

Indiana's Population

Population Density Today _____

Population Distribution Where most people live _____

Where Hoosiers Come From

What Indiana's population has done _____

People of the Distant Past First people _____

Who came to Indiana _____

People of the Recent Past More _____ and _____

Hoosiers Today Where most were born _____

Heritage How it shared _____

Religion in Indiana

Religion in the Past

1700s _____

Later _____

Religion Today

Religious groups _____

_____

_____

_____

LESSON 6 Famous Hoosiers

Vocabulary Strategies

Preteach Additional Vocabulary After teaching the Vocabulary words on Student Edition page 52, explain to students that there are several other important words they will see in this lesson. Use Procedure Card 1, along with the suggestions below, to introduce the words.

pastime	Have students give examples of pastimes, such as reading, playing sports, playing computer games, hiking, and so on.
athlete	Invite students to name athletes they know of who participate in different sports.
guitarist	Point out and pronounce the word *guitar* and the suffix *-ist*. Tell students that words with this suffix often name people. For example, a bicyclist is a person who rides a bicycle. Ask students what they think a guitarist does.
orchestra	Students may be familiar with this word but may not recognize it in print. List some other musical words in which *ch* stands for the /k/ sound, such as *choir*, *chord*, *chorus*, and *choreography*.
ballet	Ask volunteers to describe a ballet or ballet dancing. Explain that the word *ballet* is spelled and pronounced this way because it came into English from the French language.

WORD CARDS To help teach the lesson vocabulary, use the Word Cards on pages 127–128.

Build Fluency

Use page 24 and the steps on Procedure Card 2 to reinforce vocabulary and build fluency. Read each vocabulary word aloud and have students repeat it. Then have students work in pairs to reread the words. Follow a similar procedure with the phrases and sentences. Continue to help students build fluency by having them reread "You Are There" in the Student Edition.

Text Comprehension

BEFORE READING

Preview the Lesson Guide students in previewing the lesson using Procedure Card 3. Point out the following features of the lesson on Student Edition pages 52–59.

- **Pages 52–53** Read aloud the "What to Know" question. Have students recall the meaning of *culture* from Lesson 5. Preview the photograph of the Indiana State Museum on page 52 and the sports photographs on page 53. Tell students that sports are a part of Indiana's culture.

- **Pages 54–55** Preview the photographs of famous Indiana writers, poets, and artists. Tell students that the work of Indiana's authors and artists is also part of its culture.

- **Pages 56–57** Preview the photographs of famous musicians on page 56 and of Twyla Tharp and dancers on page 57. Ask whether students think that music and dance are part of culture.

- **Pages 58–59** Preview the photograph on page 58. Ask how many students have heard of David Letterman. Preview the Review questions on page 58. Call attention to the biography of Hoosier poet James Whitcomb Riley on page 59.

DURING READING

Build Comprehension of Expository Text Present the graphic organizer on page 25. Have students preview the organizer by filling in the lesson title and comparing the four main heads in the organizer with the matching subheads in the Student Edition pages 52–58. Tell students that the section subheads provide additional help with identifying important information. Use Procedure Card 4, the Reading Check questions in *Indiana Social Studies*, and the directed reading suggestions below.

- **Page 52** After students have read "You Are There," ask if anyone can name a famous Hoosier. Call attention to the names in the "People" column. Invite students to identify any names they recognize.

- **Page 53** Have students read "Sports" and make notes on the graphic organizer. Point out that the subheads in the boxes of the organizer match the section subheads in the text. Tell students to list the names of three famous Indiana basketball teams in the first box. Then they can make some brief notes about car racing and other sports in the second box.

- **Pages 54–55** After students have read "Literature and Art," have them make notes in the boxes with subheads that match the section subheads in the text. Point out that there is not enough space to list all the famous names they read about, so students should note several examples.

- **Pages 56–58** Have students read "Music" and list examples in each of the five boxes. Remind students to use the section subheads to locate information. Then students can read "Broadway and Hollywood" and again give some examples to complete the organizer. Have students compare their completed graphic organizers and explain why they chose the examples or gave the information they did.

AFTER READING

Summarize Have students use their completed graphic organizers to summarize the lesson. Then have them compare their summaries to the lesson summary on page 58.

Review and Respond Work through the Review questions with students. If students need additional help identifying main ideas and details, use Focus Skill Transparency 1.

Write a Poem Suggest that students look back over the lesson and choose a famous person they would like to write a poem about. Remind students that poems may rhyme but do not have to, though they should have rhythm and use colorful language. After students have written their poems, they may want to combine them into an anthology and give it an appropriate title.

Leveled Readers Use the Leveled Readers and Procedure Card 5 to build fluency and comprehension.

Name _____ Date _____

DIRECTIONS Read aloud the words in Part A. Practice reading aloud the phrases and the sentences in Part B.

Part A

Vocabulary Words		Additional Words	
dialect	choreographer	pastime	orchestra
science fiction		athlete	ballet
pop art		guitarist	

Part B

1. Sports / are an important pastime / for Hoosiers.

2. Some of basketball's best-known coaches / and athletes / have been from Indiana.

3. In many of his poems, / James Whitcomb Riley / used Indiana rural dialects.

4. Another Indiana writer / was Kurt Vonnegut, / who wrote science fiction.

5. Jim Davis / created the Garfield cartoon strip, / and Robert Indiana / became famous / for his pop art.

6. Wes Montgomery / was one of the greatest modern jazz guitarists.

7. Joshua Bell, / who plays the violin, / performed with a major orchestra / at the age of 14.

8. Dancer and choreographer Twyla Tharp / combines classical ballet, / tap, / and social dances.

YOU ARE THERE Turn to Student Edition page 52. Practice reading aloud "You Are There" three times. Try to improve your reading each time. Record your best time on the line below.

Number of words ___78___   My Best Time _____   Words per Minute _____

Name _____   Date _____

Lesson Title: _____

Sports

Basketball	Car Racing and More

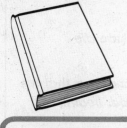

Literature and Art

Golden Age of Literature	Recent Writers	Artists

Music

Great American Songwriters	From Jazz to Opera

Pop Stars	Festivals and Concerts	Dance

Broadway and Hollywood

LESSON 1 # Early People of Indiana
Vocabulary Strategies

Preteach Additional Vocabulary After teaching the Vocabulary words on Student Edition page 76, explain to students that there are several other important words they will see in this lesson. Use Procedure Card 1, along with the suggestions below, to introduce the words.

woolly mammoth	Have students point out the woolly mammoth in the illustration on page 76. Explain that woolly mammoths lived thousands of years ago. Today, we use the word *mammoth* as a synonym for *huge* or *enormous*.
mastodon	Explain that a mastodon was another huge animal, similar to the woolly mammoth, that also lived long, long ago.
survive	Give *stay alive* and *go on* as synonyms for *survive*. Antonyms include *die* and *end*.
weapon	Students may have difficulty recognizing this word in print. Remind them that the letters *ea* can stand for the short *e* sound, as in the words *bread*, *health*, and *weather*.
site	Point out that this word, which means "place" or "location," is a homonym of *sight*.

WORD CARDS To help teach the lesson vocabulary, use the Word Cards on pages 000–000.

Build Fluency

Use page 28 and the steps on Procedure Card 2 to reinforce vocabulary and build fluency. Read each vocabulary word aloud and have students repeat it. Then have students work in pairs to reread the words. Follow a similar procedure with the phrases and sentences. Continue to help students build fluency by having them reread "You Are There" in the Student Edition.

Text Comprehension

BEFORE READING

Preview the Lesson Guide students in previewing the lesson using Procedure Card 3. Point out the following features of the lesson on Student Edition pages 76–79.

- **Pages 76–77** Read aloud the "What to Know" question. Remind students to keep this question in mind during their preview and when they read the lesson. Preview the illustration of early hunters, and the map of land routes of early people. Have students answer the map skill question. Explain briefly how a "bridge" of land formed between Asia and North America during the Ice Ages and that the bridge no longer exists.

- **Pages 78–79** Discuss the illustration of early farming on page 78 and the map of Mound-Building Cultures on page 79. Have students answer the map skill question. Then preview the Review questions.

Build Comprehension of Expository Text Present the graphic organizer on page 29. Have students preview the organizer by filling in the lesson title and comparing the three main heads in the organizer with the matching subheads in the Student Edition pages 76–79. Tell students that the section subheads provide additional help with identifying important information. Use Procedure Card 4, the Reading Check questions in *Harcourt Social Studies*, and the directed reading suggestions below.

• **Page 76** After students have read "You Are There," discuss how hunters long ago, without modern weapons, were able to kill such huge animals.

• **Page 77** Have students read "Long, Long Ago." Then guide them in writing information in the first two boxes of the graphic organizer. Point out the subheads that match the section subheads in the text, and the arrows that show that the organizer is a sequence chart or time line.

• **Page 78** After students have read "New Ways of Life," discuss the chain of causes and effects beginning with the climate change and leading eventually to forming villages. Then have students fill in the next box of the organizer. Point out that the information for this box is found in the text before the first section subhead. Students will also fill in the next box, using information found under the section subheads "New Foods" and "Settling Down and Trading."

• **Page 79** Have students read "Building Mounds" and complete the organizer. Then have a volunteer read aloud the four items in the organizer that tell "When" to confirm that the events are in sequence.

Summarize Have students use their completed graphic organizers to summarize the lesson. Then have them compare their summaries to the lesson summary on page 79.

Review and Respond Work through the Review questions with students. Use Focus Skill Transparency 2, Cause and Effect, to discuss cause and effect relationships in the lesson.

Draw Scenes Brainstorm with students some ideas for scenes they might draw. Help them determine the approximate time period for each scene. Then each student can choose two scenes from different times in history. Display the completed drawings in a time line format, grouping drawings from each time period.

Leveled Readers Use the Leveled Readers and Procedure Card 5 to build fluency and comprehension.

Name _____ Date _____

Part A

Vocabulary Words		Additional Words	
nomad	mound	woolly mammoth	weapon
ancestor	permanent	mastodon	site
extinct	barter	survive	

Part B

1. The ancestors / of present-day Native Americans / were nomads.

2. They used spears / tipped with stone points / to hunt mastodons / and woolly mammoths.

3. When the last Ice Age ended, / the warmer climate / caused the larger animals / to become extinct.

4. People / had to change their ways of life / to survive.

5. As a result of agriculture, / Native Americans / began building permanent shelters / and staying in one place.

6. Native Americans / used boats / to travel long distances / to barter.

7. They got items / such as seashells and copper, / which they used / to make better tools / and weapons.

8. Woodland Indians, / who lived in Indiana / about 3,000 years ago, / are known for building mounds.

9. Some mounds / were burial places, / home building sites, / and trading centers.

YOU ARE THERE Turn to Student Edition page 76. Practice reading aloud "You Are There" three times. Try to improve your reading each time. Record your best time on the line below.

Number of words ___72___   My Best Time _____   Words per Minute _____

Name _____ Date _____

Lesson Title: _____

Long, Long Ago

Early People Arrive Called _____

⬇

Early People of Indiana When _____

⬇

New Ways of Life

Why _____

⬇

New Foods Who _____ Foods _____

_____

Settling Down and Trading When _____

What Native Americans did _____

_____

⬇

Building Mounds

When _____ Who _____

What they did _____

⬇

Angel Mounds When _____

Who _____ How many mounds _____

LESSON 2 # Native Peoples of Indiana

Vocabulary Strategies

Preteach Additional Vocabulary After teaching the Vocabulary words on Student Edition page 82, explain to students that there are several other important words they will see in this lesson. Use Procedure Card 1, along with the suggestions below, to introduce the words.

prairie	Tell students that prairies are areas of mostly flat grasslands.
buffalo	Display a picture of a buffalo. Tell students that years ago, huge herds of buffalo lived on the Midwestern plains.
council	Tell students that a council is a group of people who are chosen to decide on laws or rules for their community. Read this context sentence: "A council of older men and women helped chiefs make decisions."
healer	Have students identify the base word *heal* and suffix *-er*. A healer is a person who heals, or makes people well again when they are sick or hurt. Have students give other examples of words with the same suffix, such as *teacher*, *farmer*, and *singer*.
sap	Ask whether students have ever had maple syrup on pancakes or waffles. Discuss briefly how maple syrup is made from the sap, or fluid, from maple trees.

WORD CARDS To help teach the lesson vocabulary, use the Word Cards on pages 000–000.

Build Fluency

Use page 32 and the steps on Procedure Card 2 to reinforce vocabulary and build fluency. Read each vocabulary word aloud and have students repeat it. Then have students work in pairs to reread the words. Follow a similar procedure with the phrases and sentences. Continue to help students build fluency by having them reread "You Are There" in the Student Edition.

Text Comprehension

BEFORE READING

Preview the Lesson Guide students in previewing the lesson using Procedure Card 3. Point out the following features of the lesson on Student Edition pages 82–89.

- **Pages 82–83** Read aloud the "What to Know" question. Point out the names of early Native American groups on the time line at the top of the page. Have students examine and discuss the illustration of a Miami village and the map of Indiana's Native American tribes. Then have students answer the map skill question.

- **Pages 84–85** Have students read the Children in History feature about Miami children and discuss the Make It Relevant question. Preview the illustration of a Shawnee village on page 85. Have students compare it to the Miami village pictured on pages 82–83 and use the map to find where the Shawnee lived.

- **Pages 86–87** Preview the photographs of the Lenape Indian Camp at the Connor Prairie History Museum and the Lenape deerskin bag on page 86. Have students read the Primary Sources feature about lacrosse and discuss the Document-Based Question.

- **Pages 88–89** Preview the photographs of Indiana artifacts on page 88. On page 89, preview the photograph of a Native American storyteller and then the Review questions.

DURING READING

Build Comprehension of Expository Text Present the graphic organizer on page 33. Have students preview the organizer by filling in the lesson title and comparing the six main heads in the organizer with the matching subheads in the Student Edition pages 82–89. Tell students that the section subheads provide additional help with identifying important information. Use Procedure Card 4, the Reading Check questions in *Harcourt Social Studies*, and the directed reading suggestions below.

- **Page 82** After students have read "You Are There," have them point out in the illustration the various activities described in the passage. Discuss how people's lives today are similar to and different from the lives of these people.

- **Page 83** Before students read "Tribes and Culture," have them look at the first box of the organizer to set a purpose for reading. After reading, have students locate the date given at the beginning of the section. Then guide them in identifying and writing a main idea sentence for each subsection.

- **Pages 84–86** Have students use the organizer to set a purpose for reading the next section, "The Miami." Point out that there is only enough space in the organizer to write the most important details. After students have read this section and filled in the box, follow a similar procedure for the next section, "The Shawnee." Then do the same for "The Lenape."

- **Pages 87–89** Before students read "The Potawatomi," have them use the organizer to set a purpose for reading. Point out that students will write a main idea sentence for each subsection. After filling in that box, follow a similar procedure to have students read "Learning from the Past" and complete the organizer.

AFTER READING

Summarize Have students use their completed graphic organizers to summarize the lesson. Then have them compare their summaries to the lesson summary on page 89.

Review and Respond Work through the Review questions with students. If students need additional help identifying cause and effect relationships, use Focus Skill Transparency 2.

Write a Story Have students name some landforms and bodies of water in Indiana and choose items from this list to write about. Students may need to do a bit of research to learn more about the shape, size, or other features of the landform or body of water. After they have written their legends, students may enjoy taking turns as the "storyteller" and reading their work aloud.

Leveled Readers Use the Leveled Readers and Procedure Card 5 to build fluency and comprehension.

Name _____ Date _____

Read aloud the words in Part A. Practice reading aloud the phrases and the sentences in Part B.

Part A

Vocabulary Words		Additional Words	
historic	clan	prairie	sap
tribe	artifact	buffalo	
specialize	legend	council	
longhouse		healer	

Part B

1. By 1650, / groups known as the Historic Indians / lived in Indiana.

2. Some Native Americans / formed groups called tribes.

3. On the nearby prairies, / Native Americans / hunted buffalo.

4. A council of older men and women / helped chiefs of Miami villages / make decisions.

5. Some Miami people / could specialize in jobs / such as making pots / or weaving.

6. Some Shawnee families / were healers.

7. The Lenape / lived in wigwams / and longhouses.

8. The Lenape / made maple sugar / from maple tree sap.

9. Every Potawatomi person / belonged to a clan.

10. Much of what we know / about Native Americans in Indiana / comes from artifacts and legends.

YOU ARE THERE **Turn to Student Edition page 82. Practice reading aloud "You Are There" three times. Try to improve your reading each time. Record your best time on the line below.**

Number of words ___50___   My Best Time _____   Words per Minute _____

Name _____ Date _____

Lesson Title: _____

Tribes and Culture

When _____

Forming Tribes   Main Idea _____

_____

Environment and Culture   Main

Idea _____

_____

The Miami

Village Life   Important Details

_____

_____

_____

_____

The Shawnee

Trading and Hunting   Details

_____

_____

Community Life   Details _____

_____

The Lenape

When _____

Ways of Life   Details _____

_____

_____

The Potawatomi

Using Resources   Main Idea _____

_____

Living in Groups   Main Idea _____

_____

Learning from the Past

Artifacts   Main Idea _____

_____

Storytelling   Main Idea _____

_____

_____

LESSON 3 **Exploration and Settlement**

Vocabulary Strategies

Preteach Additional Vocabulary After teaching the Vocabulary words on Student Edition page 92, explain to students that there are several other important words they will see in this lesson. Use Procedure Card 1, along with the suggestions below, to introduce the words.

route	Ask volunteers to describe the route between their homes and school.
claim	Explain that when an explorer claimed land for a country, it meant that the country now owned that land.
founded	Tell students that in addition to its usual meaning, *found* can also mean to start something, such as a new colony. The *-ed* ending is added to show that the action took place in the past.
trading post	Discuss familiar meanings of *post*, such as fence post and post office. Explain that years ago a trading post was a kind of store where people could buy, sell, and trade goods.
conflict	Tell students that *conflict* has many synonyms, including *disagreement*, *tension*, *quarrel*, *argument*, *fight*, *struggle*, *battle*, and *war*. Discuss the concept of connotation, pointing out that some of these synonyms are stronger words than others. Explain that students can use the context to determine which synonym fits.

WORD CARDS To help teach the lesson vocabulary, use the Word Cards on pages 000–000.

Build Fluency

Use page 36 and the steps on Procedure Card 2 to reinforce vocabulary and build fluency. Read each vocabulary word aloud and have students repeat it. Then have students work in pairs to reread the words. Follow a similar procedure with the phrases and sentences. Continue to help students build fluency by having them reread "You Are There" in the Student Edition.

Text Comprehension

BEFORE READING

Preview the Lesson Guide students in previewing the lesson using Procedure Card 3. Point out the following features of the lesson on Student Edition pages 92–97.

• **Pages 92–93** Read aloud the "What to Know" question. Preview the time line, the photograph of the replica of a French fort on page 92, and the illustration of Columbus's ships on page 93.

• **Pages 94–95** Preview the illustration of fur trading between Native Americans and Europeans. Explain that the Europeans wanted furs to send back to Europe, where they sold for high prices. Native Americans wanted tools, knives, and other European goods. Have students examine the table and answer the question in the caption.

- **Pages 96–97** Preview the painting of a French and Indian War battle on page 96. Explain that this war was fought between the French and the British, with Native American allies on both sides. On page 97, preview the image of the Proclamation of 1763 and the portrait of Chief Pontiac. Then preview the Review questions.

DURING READING

Build Comprehension of Expository Text Present the graphic organizer on page 37. Have students preview the organizer by filling in the lesson title and comparing the four main heads in the organizer with the matching subheads in the Student Edition pages 92–97. Tell students that the section subheads provide additional help with identifying important information. Use Procedure Card 4, the Reading Check questions in *Harcourt Social Studies*, and the directed reading suggestions below.

- **Page 92** After students have read "You Are There," have volunteers role play a Native American and a French fur trader. Ask each of them: *What did you bring to trade? What will you get in return?*

- **Page 93** Have students read "Exploring the Americas." Discuss the effects of Columbus's adventures on other explorers, and the effects of European exploration on Native Americans. Then have students fill in the first box in the graphic organizer. Point out the two subheads that match the section subheads in the text.

- **Page 94** After students have read "Exploring Indiana," have them locate on a map the places that La Salle explored. Then have them fill in the next box in the organizer.

- **Pages 95–97** Have students read "The Fur Trade" and fill in the corresponding box in the organizer. Point out that some information will be found in the text before the section subhead "Trade Grows." Then students can read "War over Land" and complete the organizer.

AFTER READING

Summarize Have students use their completed graphic organizers to summarize the lesson. Then have them compare their summaries to the lesson summary on page 97.

Review and Respond Work through the Review questions with students. If students need additional help identifying cause and effect relationships, use Focus Skill Transparency 2.

Write a Persuasive Letter Discuss with students their purpose in writing this letter, the opinion they wish to express, and how they might support that opinion. You may want to provide a model of the correct form for a business letter.

Leveled Readers Use the Leveled Readers and Procedure Card 5 to build fluency and comprehension.

Name _____ Date _____

Read aloud the words in Part A. Practice reading aloud the phrases and the sentences in Part B.

Part A

Vocabulary Words		Additional Words
explorer	voyageur	route
colony	allies	claim
expedition	treaty	founded
missionary	proclamation	trading post
scarce		conflict

Part B

1. In 1492, / explorer Christopher Columbus / left Spain / to find a sea route to Asia.

2. In the early 1600s, / the French / had founded a colony / called New France.

3. La Salle, / a French explorer, / led an expedition / into what is now Indiana.

4. The arrival of French traders / and missionaries / changed the way / Native Americans lived.

5. Furs from beavers /and other animals / sold for high prices in Europe, / where they were scarce.

6. Voyageurs / took the furs to Montreal / to be shipped to Europe.

7. The French / built trading posts / protected by soldiers / in what is now / Indiana.

8. British colonists / wanted to settle lands / in the Ohio Valley / that the French had already claimed.

9. Most Native Americans / were allies of the French, / but a part of the Miami tribe / signed a treaty / with the British.

10. To avoid further conflicts, / King George III of Britain/ issued a proclamation.

YOU ARE THERE Turn to Student Edition page 92. Practice reading aloud "You Are There" three times. Try to improve your reading each time. Record your best time on the line below.

Number of words ___75___ My Best Time _____ Words per Minute _____

Name _____ Date _____

Lesson Title: _____

Exploring the Americas

Looking for a Route to Asia   When _____   Who _____

Arriving in the Americas   What European explorers did _____

_____

Exploring Indiana

French Explorers   First to visit Indiana _____   When _____

The Fur Trade

Who came to Indiana _____ and _____

Trade Grows   Where furs were sold _____

What European traders offered _____

Effect on Native Americans _____

War over Land

Forts and Trading Posts   First permanent European settlement in Indiana _____

_____ When _____ Where _____

The French and Indian War   Began _____ Ended _____

What Britain gained _____

LESSON 4 **The American Revolution**

Vocabulary Strategies

Preteach Additional Vocabulary After teaching the Vocabulary words on Student Edition page 100, explain to students that there are several other important words they will see in this lesson. Use Procedure Card 1, along with the suggestions below, to introduce the words.

representation	Point out the word *represent* and suffix *-ation*, which has the same meaning as the suffix *-tion*, "action or process." Explain that people have representation when someone represents, or speaks for, them.
base	Tell students that *base* has multiple meanings. Have them use the context to determine its meaning in this sentence: "Britain's main base in the West was Fort Detroit, in what is now Michigan."
loyalty	Cover the suffix *-ty* and have students identify the word *loyal*. Invite them to tell why loyalty is an important quality in a friend.
cause	Discuss familiar meanings of *cause*, such as in the phrase *cause and effect*. Tell students that a cause can also be an idea that people believe in and fight for.
recapture	Write *capture* and *recapture*. If necessary, remind students that the prefix *re-* means "again" or "back." Other words with this prefix include *rebuild*, *repay*, and *replace*.

WORD CARDS To help teach the lesson vocabulary, use the Word Cards on pages 000–000.

Build Fluency

Use page 40 and the steps on Procedure Card 2 to reinforce vocabulary and build fluency. Read each vocabulary word aloud and have students repeat it. Then have students work in pairs to reread the words. Follow a similar procedure with the phrases and sentences. Continue to help students build fluency by having them reread "You Are There" in the Student Edition.

Text Comprehension

BEFORE READING

Preview the Lesson Guide students in previewing the lesson using Procedure Card 3. Point out the following features of the lesson on Student Edition pages 100–105.

• **Pages 100–101** Read aloud the "What to Know" question. Preview the time line and the painting of the Boston Tea Party on pages 100–101. Have students read and discuss the Fast Fact.

• **Pages 102–103** Point out the small photograph of soldier gear from the American Revolution on page 102. Have students examine the illustrated map on page 103 and trace Clark's and Hamilton's routes.

- **Pages 104–105** Preview the photograph of the Yorktown victory monument and the Review questions on page 104. Call attention to the biography of George Rogers Clark on page 105. Have students recall what they learned about Clark in their preview of page 103.

DURING READING

Build Comprehension of Expository Text Present the graphic organizer on page 41. Have students preview the organizer by filling in the lesson title and comparing the three main heads in the organizer with the matching subheads in the Student Edition pages 100–104. Tell students that the section subheads provide additional help with identifying important information. Use Procedure Card 4, the Reading Check questions in *Harcourt Social Studies*, and the directed reading suggestions below.

- **Page 100** After students have read "You Are There," discuss the reasons the father is upset. Ask whether students think other colonists may also be upset about these issues.

- **Page 101** Have students read "A War for Freedom" and discuss the events that led up to the war. Then have students fill in the first box of the graphic organizer. Explain that they will have to summarize events very briefly to tell what happened. Point out the two subheads that match the section subheads in the text.

- **Page 102** After students have read "The War in Indiana," have them discuss the events they read about and then fill in the next box in the organizer. Remind them to use the four section subheads to locate information in the text.

- **Pages 103–104** Have students read "The War Ends" and complete the organizer.

AFTER READING

Summarize Have students use their completed graphic organizers to summarize the lesson. Then have them compare their summaries to the lesson summary on page 104.

Review and Respond Work through the Review questions with students. If students need additional help identifying cause and effect relationships, use Focus Skill Transparency 2.

Draw a Cartoon Discuss briefly with students the art and purpose of political cartooning. You may want to provide and analyze several examples. After students have drawn their own cartoons, they can use them to create a classroom display.

Leveled Readers Use the Leveled Readers and Procedure Card 5 to build fluency and comprehension.

Name _____ Date _____

DIRECTIONS Read aloud the words in Part A. Practice reading aloud the phrases and the sentences in Part B.

Part A

Vocabulary Words		Additional Words	
tax	militia	representation	cause
independence	surrender	base	recapture
revolution		loyalty	

Part B

1. In 1765, / the British government / passed a law / that placed a tax / on paper goods / in the colonies.

2. Many colonists / did not want to pay these taxes / because they did not have representation / in the British government.

3. Some colonists / began to call for independence, / and anger / turned to war.

4. The colonists' war for independence / is called the American Revolution.

5. Britain's main base in the West / was Fort Detroit, / in what is today / Michigan.

6. George Rogers Clark / of Kentucky / led the Kentucky militia.

7. After Clark and his soldiers / captured a fort at Kaskaskia, / villagers in the nearby French settlement / promised loyalty to Clark.

8. Father Gibault, / a Jesuit priest, / convinced the French citizens of Vincennes / to support the American cause.

9. When Clark / led a surprise attack / to recapture Fort Sackville, / the leader there / decided to surrender.

You Are There Turn to Student Edition page 100. Practice reading aloud "You Are There" three times. Try to improve your reading each time. Record your best time on the line below.

Number of words ___78___ My Best Time _____ Words per Minute _____

Name _____ Date _____

Lesson Title: _____

<table>
<tr><td>

A War for Freedom

Anger over Taxes

What happened _____

_____

How colonists felt _____

_____

Why _____

_____

The Revolution Begins

What colonists wanted _____

When war began _____

</td><td>

The War in Indiana

Native Americans Join the Fight

Why _____

_____

The Settlers Fight Back

Who _____

What he planned to do _____

_____

_____

_____

Clark's Army

What they did _____

Fort Sackville

What happened _____

_____

_____

</td></tr>
</table>

The War Ends

When _____ How _____

_____

_____ Who had won _____

LESSON 5 **The Northwest Territory**

Vocabulary Strategies

Preteach Additional Vocabulary After teaching the Vocabulary words on Student Edition page 108, explain to students that there are several other important words they will see in this lesson. Use Procedure Card 1, along with the suggestions below, to introduce the words.

recognize	Discuss the meaning of *recognize* in this context: "In 1763, the British and the Americans signed a second Treaty of Paris. It recognized the United States of America as a new country."
appointed	Explain that some officials, such as the President and Congress, are elected by the people. Other officials are appointed, or chosen, to do a particular task.
former	Have students name some former Presidents of the United States.
unite	Tell students that *unite* is from the Latin word *unus*, which means "one." When people unite, they join together in one group. Other words from this root include *unit*, *union*, and *unity*.
armed	Ask students to raise their arms. Explain that the word *arm* comes from the Latin word *armus*, or "shoulder." To arm someone means to give someone a weapon or weapons. This meaning of *arm* comes from the Latin word *arma*, "weapons."

WORD CARDS To help teach the lesson vocabulary, use the Word Cards on pages 000–000.

Build Fluency

Use page 44 and the steps on Procedure Card 2 to reinforce vocabulary and build fluency. Read each vocabulary word aloud and have students repeat it. Then have students work in pairs to reread the words. Follow a similar procedure with the phrases and sentences. Continue to help students build fluency by having them reread "You Are There" in the Student Edition.

Text Comprehension

BEFORE READING

Preview the Lesson Guide students in previewing the lesson using Procedure Card 3. Point out the following features of the lesson on Student Edition pages 108–113.

• **Pages 108–109** Read aloud the "What to Know" question. Tell students that as they learn about the Northwest Ordinance, they should remember to think about how it affected settlers and Native Americans. Preview the time line and the photograph of the George Rogers Clark Memorial on page 108. Have students recall what they have learned about Clark and Fort Sackville. Then have them read the Children in History feature about Frances Slocum and discuss the Make It Relevant question.

• **Pages 110–111** Have students examine and discuss the map of the Northwest Territory on page 110 and answer the map skill question. Preview the painting of the signing of the Treaty of Greenville on page 111. Explain that by signing this treaty, Native Americans gave up most of their land in the Northwest Territory.

- **Pages 112–113** Preview the painting that shows the signing of the Treaty of Ghent. Then preview the Review questions on page 112. Call attention to the biography of Tecumseh on page 113. Remind students that they are going to learn how the Northwest Ordinance affected settlers and how it affected Native Americans like the Shawnee leader Tecumseh and his people.

DURING READING

Build Comprehension of Expository Text Present the graphic organizer on page 45. Have students preview the organizer by filling in the lesson title and comparing the two main heads in the organizer with the matching subheads in the Student Edition pages 108–112. Tell students that the section subheads provide additional help with identifying important information. Use Procedure Card 4, the Reading Check questions in *Harcourt Social Studies*, and the directed reading suggestions below.

- **Page 108** After students have read "You Are There," ask whether they think paying the soldiers by giving them land is a good idea, and why or why not.

- **Page 109** Have students read "Expanding West" and write information in the sequence chart on the graphic organizer page. Point out that there are two boxes in the organizer for this section of the lesson. Information for the first box will be found in the text under the main head "Expanding West." Information for the second box will be found under the section subhead "A New Territory."

- **Pages 110–112** As students read "Settling the Northwest Territory," you may want to have them pause to fill in information in each box before they read on. Point out that the information for the first box is found under the main heading in the text. The subheads in the remaining boxes match the section subheads in the text. After students complete the organizer, have them check the dates to verify that the events are in time order.

AFTER READING

Summarize Have students use their completed graphic organizers to summarize the lesson. Then have them compare their summaries to the lesson summary on page 112.

Review and Respond Work through the Review questions with students. If students need additional help identifying cause and effect relationships, use Focus Skill Transparency 2.

Write a Newspaper Editorial Remind students that a newspaper editorial states an opinion. Have students suggest varying opinions that newspaper editors might have had about the conflicts over land in the Northwest Territory. Tell students to choose a point of view for the editorial they will write. Remind them to use facts from the lesson to support their opinions.

Leveled Readers Use the Leveled Readers and Procedure Card 5 to build fluency and comprehension.

Name _____ Date _____

DIRECTIONS Read aloud the words in Part A. Practice reading aloud the phrases and the sentences in Part B.

Part A

Vocabulary Words		Additional Words	
debt	township	recognize	unite
territory	right	appointed	armed
ordinance		former	

Part B

1. The British and the Americans / signed a treaty / that recognized the United States of America / as a new country.

2. Congress / decided to use lands / west of the Appalachians / to help pay debts.

3. The area north of the Ohio River / became known as / the Northwest Territory.

4. The Land Ordinance of 1785 / divided the land into squares / called townships.

5. The Northwest Ordinance of 1787 / promised settlers / freedom of religion / and various legal and property rights.

6. Congress appointed / former general Arthur St. Clair, / who fought in the American Revolution, / governor of the Northwest Territory.

7. Two Shawnee leaders / urged Native Americans / to unite / against the settlers.

8. Many people / thought that the British / had armed Native Americans / to fight the settlers.

YOU ARE THERE Turn to Student Edition page 108. Practice reading aloud "You Are There" three times. Try to improve your reading each time. Record your best time on the line below.

Number of words ____73____   My Best Time _____   Words per Minute _____

Name _____ Date _____

Lesson Title: _____

Expanding West
Date _____ New country _____

A New Territory
Where _____

Settling the Northwest Territory
What Congress passed _____
What it did _____

The Northwest Ordinance
Date _____ What the law set up _____

Conflicts over Land
Why _____   _____
Outcome _____   _____

The Indiana Territory
Date _____ First governor _____ Capital _____

The War of 1812
War between _____ Ended _____

LESSON 6 **A New State**

Vocabulary Strategies

Preteach Additional Vocabulary After teaching the Vocabulary words on Student Edition page 118, explain to students that there are several other important words they will see in this lesson. Use Procedure Card 1, along with the suggestions below, to introduce the words.

statehood	Have students identify the word *state* and suffix *-hood*. Explain that statehood is the condition of being a state.
supreme	Give these examples: The supreme court of Indiana is the highest and most powerful court in our state. The United States Supreme Court is the highest and most powerful court in our nation.
basic	Discuss the idea that a base, such as the base of a lamp, is very important because the lamp could not stand up without it. Something that is basic is like a base. A basic right is so important that people's freedom depends on it.
disagree	Have students identify the word *agree* and prefix *dis-*. Explain that *dis-* can mean "do the opposite." *Agree* and *disagree* are antonyms.
revise	Talk with students about why we revise as part of the writing process. (to add details we left out, to take out details we do not need, to express ideas more clearly, etc.)

WORD CARDS To help teach the lesson vocabulary, use the Word Cards on pages 000–000.

Build Fluency

Use page 48 and the steps on Procedure Card 2 to reinforce vocabulary and build fluency. Read each vocabulary word aloud and have students repeat it. Then have students work in pairs to reread the words. Follow a similar procedure with the phrases and sentences. Continue to help students build fluency by having them reread "You Are There" in the Student Edition.

Text Comprehension

BEFORE READING

Preview the Lesson Guide students in previewing the lesson using Procedure Card 3. Point out the following features of the lesson on Student Edition pages 118–121.

• **Pages 118–119** Read aloud the "What to Know" question. Preview the time line, and ask students what they can learn from it about the new state. Then preview the illustration of the Constitution Elm and the photograph of the Harrison County Courthouse, both in Corydon, Indiana's first state capital.

• **Pages 120–121** Call attention to the illustrated time line of the Road to Statehood. Discuss briefly how each event or item on the time line contributes to a better understanding of how Indiana became a state. Preview the Review questions on page 121.

Build Comprehension of Expository Text Present the graphic organizer on page 49. Have students preview the organizer by filling in the lesson title and comparing the two main heads in the organizer with the matching subheads in the Student Edition pages 118–121. Tell students that the section subheads provide additional help with identifying important information. Use Procedure Card 4, the Reading Check questions in *Harcourt Social Studies*, and the directed reading suggestions below.

- **Page 118** After students have read "You Are There," point out that the illustration on this page shows the scene described in the passage. Ask students what kind of plan they think was made for Indiana's government.

- **Page 119** Before students read "Statehood for Indiana," have them look at the graphic organizer to set a purpose for reading this section of the lesson. Then have students read the section and list in the organizer the five steps described in the text under the section subhead "Steps Toward Statehood."

- **Pages 120–121** Now have students read "The Nineteenth State" and fill in the second box in the organizer. Point out the blanks for two dates that students will find in the text under the main section head. Remind students to use the three section subheads to help them find the rest of the information to complete the organizer.

AFTER READING

Summarize Have students use their completed graphic organizers to summarize the lesson. Then have them compare their summaries to the lesson summary on page 121.

Review and Respond Work through the Review questions with students. If students need additional help identifying cause and effect relationships, use Focus Skill Transparency 2.

Make a Flowchart Discuss with students what a flowchart is and how to construct one. Suggest that students determine what steps to show by looking back at page 119 in the text and also at the first box they completed in the graphic organizer for this lesson.

Leveled Readers Use the Leveled Readers and Procedure Card 5 to build fluency and comprehension.

Name _____ Date _____

Part A

Vocabulary Words		Additional Words	
census	constitution	statehood	disagree
enabling act	slavery	supreme	revise
delegate	illegal	basic	

Part B

1. The 1815 census / showed Indiana's population / to be more than 63,000 free adults / —enough to apply for statehood.

2. In April 1816, / President James Madison / signed the enabling act / into law.

3. The enabling act / called for voters / to elect delegates / to attend a convention.

4. The Indiana Constitution of 1816 / established the first state government.

5. Like today's government, / it was made up of the governor, / General Assembly, / and state supreme court.

6. The Indiana Constitution of 1816 / promised to protect / the basic rights / of the people.

7. The delegates / disagreed / about the issue of slavery.

8. Finally, / the delegates voted / to make slavery illegal / in Indiana.

9. In 1851, / voters decided / that the constitution / needed to be revised.

 Turn to Student Edition page 118. Practice reading aloud "You Are There" three times. Try to improve your reading each time. Record your best time on the line below.

Number of words ___72___ My Best Time _____ Words per Minute _____

Name _____ Date _____

Lesson Title: _____

Statehood for Indiana

Steps Toward Statehood

1. _____
2. _____
3. _____
4. _____
5. _____

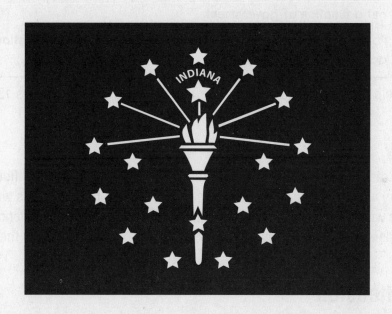

The Nineteenth State

Constitution date _____ Statehood date _____

A Plan for Government   What it established _____

Promised to protect _____

Indiana Leaders   First governor _____ Capital _____

A New Constitution   What voters decided _____

Constitution that is still in use today _____

Unit 3

LESSON 1 New Communities

Vocabulary Strategies

Preteach Additional Vocabulary After teaching the Vocabulary words on Student Edition page 140, explain to students that there are several other important words they will see in this lesson. Use Procedure Card 1, along with the suggestions below, to introduce the words.

opposition	Write *oppose, opposite,* and *opposition,* and have students compare the words. Discuss this sentence: "They were drawn to Indiana by the state's fertile farmland and opposition to slavery."
pioneer	Tell students that a pioneer is a person who comes to settle a new place.
self-sufficient	Have students use context clues: "Trade was difficult, so families had to be self-sufficient. Pioneers hunted and grew their own food. They also made their own clothes, furniture, and medicine."
commission	Explain that a commission is a group of people who perform a duty or carry out a function of government.
removal	Point out the word *remove* and suffix *-al,* which means "action." Removal is the action of removing something.

WORD CARDS To help teach the lesson vocabulary, use the Word Cards on pages 137–138.

Build Fluency

Use page 52 and the steps on Procedure Card 2 to reinforce vocabulary and build fluency. Read each vocabulary word aloud and have students repeat it. Then have students work in pairs to reread the words. Follow a similar procedure with the phrases and sentences. Continue to help students build fluency by having them reread "You Are There" in the Student Edition.

Text Comprehension

BEFORE READING

Preview the Lesson Guide students in previewing the lesson using Procedure Card 3. Point out the following features of the lesson on Student Edition pages 140–147.

- **Pages 140–141** Read aloud the "What to Know" question, and invite students to suggest some possible answers. Preview the time line and the illustration of early settlers crossing the Ohio River. Have students read the Children in History feature about Abraham Lincoln on page 141 and discuss the Make It Relevant question.

- **Pages 142–143** Preview the illustrated time line "Indiana Grows" and discuss what it shows about the growth of Indiana from 1814 to 1850.

- **Pages 144–145** Have students examine the illustration "Transportation in Indiana" and identify the three different forms of transportation it shows. Discuss the question in the caption.

- **Pages 146–147** Preview the painting and the Review questions on page 146. Call attention to the biography of Robert Owen on page 147. Tell students that Owen started the town of New Harmony in Indiana.

DURING READING

Build Comprehension of Expository Text Present the graphic organizer on page 53. Have students preview the organizer by filling in the lesson title and comparing the four main heads in the organizer with the matching subheads in the Student Edition pages 140–146. Tell students that the section subheads provide additional help with identifying important information. Use Procedure Card 4, the Reading Check questions in *Indiana Social Studies*, and the directed reading suggestions below.

- **Page 140** After students have read "You Are There," ask them to list the positive and negative points about leaving Kentucky to settle in Indiana.

- **Page 141** Have students read "A Thriving State" and fill in the first box of the organizer. Point out the two subheads that match the section subheads in the text.

- **Pages 142–143** After students have read "Growing Communities," have them fill in the second box in the organizer. Remind them to use the section subheads to help locate information.

- **Pages 144–145** Have students read "Transportation." Discuss briefly how and why methods of transportation changed and why transportation is important to the economy. Then have students use the four section subheads in the text to locate information and write it in the organizer.

- **Page 146** After reading and briefly discussing "Indian Removal," students can complete the organizer.

AFTER READING

Summarize Have students use their completed graphic organizers to summarize the lesson. Then have them compare their summaries to the lesson summary on page 146.

Review and Respond Work through the Review questions with students. Use Focus Skill Transparency 3, Summarize, to guide students in summarizing the lesson.

Make an Advertisement Suggest that students reread the passage in the text that tells about the community of New Harmony. Remind students that an advertisement tries to persuade people to do something. Discuss ideas that students might use in their advertisements to persuade people to move to New Harmony.

Leveled Readers Use the Leveled Readers and Procedure Card 5 to build fluency and comprehension.

Name _____ Date _____

DIRECTIONS Read aloud the words in Part A. Practice reading aloud the phrases and the sentences in Part B.

Part A

Vocabulary Words		Additional Words	
migration	navigable	opposition	commission
flatboat	stagecoach	pioneer	removal
steamboat		self-sufficient	

Part B

1. The migration / of thousands of Americans / to Indiana / and other lands west of the Appalachian Mountains / took place / in the early 1800s.

2. The Quakers / were drawn to Indiana / by the state's fertile farmland / and opposition to slavery.

3. Pioneers / came to Indiana / by horse and wagon / or traveled in rafts / down the Ohio River.

4. Trade / was difficult, / so families / had to be self-sufficient.

5. In 1820, / a commission / chose an area / in the center of the state / to be the new state capital.

6. Early pioneers / used flatboats / to take goods to market / and to carry people.

7. Later, / steamboats traveled up and down / navigable rivers.

8. Wagons and stagecoaches / carried people and goods / along new roads.

9. Because of the Indian Removal Act, / more than 800 Potawatomi / were forced to leave Indiana.

 Turn to Student Edition page 140. Practice reading aloud "You Are There" three times. Try to improve your reading each time. Record your best time on the line below.

Number of words ___84___ My Best Time _____ Words per Minute _____

Name _____ Date _____

Lesson Title: _____

<table>
<tr>
<td>

A Thriving State

Population Growth Why _____

_____

Pioneers Come to Indiana Who

_____

_____

_____

</td>
<td>

Growing Communities

New Harmony What it was _____

_____

The Formation of Counties Why

_____

Indianapolis Where _____

_____

</td>
</tr>
</table>

Transportation

Steamboats Invented by _____ When _____

Canals How they improved the economy _____

_____

How they hurt the economy _____

Roads What they did _____

Railroads What they did _____

Indian Removal

Why _____

What happened _____

LESSON 2 **The Civil War**

Vocabulary Strategies

Preteach Additional Vocabulary After teaching the Vocabulary words on Student Edition page 150, explain to students that there are several other important words they will see in this lesson. Use Procedure Card 1, along with the suggestions below, to introduce the words.

balance	Invite students to give meanings they know for this word. Draw or display a balance scale and point out that there is a balance when the two sides are equal.
politician	Ask whether students can name some politicians, or people who work in government, such as the President, governor, senators, mayor, and so on.
runaway	Have students identify the two shorter words, *run* and *away*, that make up this compound word. Then ask why students think a person might be called a runaway.
conductor	Ask students to describe the job of a conductor on a train. Explain that although the Underground Railroad was not an actual railroad, the people who helped runaways escape were called conductors.
emancipation	Explain that emancipation is the act of setting someone free. The Emancipation Proclamation gave freedom to enslaved people in the Confederate states at the time of the Civil War.

WORD CARDS To help teach the lesson vocabulary, use the Word Cards on pages 137–138.

Build Fluency

Use page 56 and the steps on Procedure Card 2 to reinforce vocabulary and build fluency. Read each vocabulary word aloud and have students repeat it. Then have students work in pairs to reread the words. Follow a similar procedure with the phrases and sentences. Continue to help students build fluency by having them reread "You Are There" in the Student Edition.

Text Comprehension

BEFORE READING

Preview the Lesson Guide students in previewing the lesson using Procedure Card 3. Point out the following features of the lesson on Student Edition pages 150–157.

• **Pages 150–151** Read aloud the "What to Know" question. Preview the time line and the illustration of people escaping slavery. Remind students that many enslaved people escaped by way of the Underground Railroad. Have students examine the map of Civil War states on page 151 and answer the map skill questions.

- **Pages 152–153** Preview the cutaway illustration of an Underground Railroad station on pages 152 and 153. Discuss the question in the caption.

- **Pages 154–155** Preview the photographs of Indiana soldiers on page 154 and the painting of Morgan's Raiders on page 155. Tell students that Morgan was a Confederate general who won a battle against Union troops in Indiana.

- **Pages 156–157** Preview the painting and the Review questions on page 156. Call attention to the biography of Indiana abolitionists Levi and Catharine Coffin on page 157.

DURING READING

Build Comprehension of Expository Text Present the graphic organizer on page 57. Have students preview the organizer by filling in the lesson title and comparing the three main heads in the organizer with the matching subheads in the Student Edition pages 150-156. Tell students that the section subheads provide additional help with identifying important information. Use Procedure Card 4, the Reading Check questions in *Indiana Social Studies*, and the directed reading suggestions below.

- **Page 150** After students have read "You Are There," discuss what the runaway family described in the passage might have been thinking and feeling as they proceeded on their journey.

- **Page 151** Have students read "North and South." Discuss the main points from this section of the lesson. Then have students fill in the first box in the graphic organizer. Point out that some information can be found in the text before the section subhead "The Issue of Slavery."

- **Pages 152–153** After students have read "Indiana Abolitionists," discuss briefly the various methods used by different abolitionists and groups of abolitionists in the fight against slavery. Then have students fill in the second box in the organizer. Remind them to use the three section subheads to locate information in the text.

- **Pages 154–156** Have students read and discuss briefly "The Civil War in Indiana." Then have them use the four section subheads in the text to locate information and complete the organizer.

AFTER READING

Summarize Have students use their completed graphic organizers to summarize the lesson. Then have them compare their summaries to the lesson summary on page 156.

Review and Respond Work through the Review questions with students. If students need additional help with summarizing, use Focus Skill Transparency 3.

Write a Report Provide or suggest appropriate print resources, and also discuss with students keywords they might use for an Internet search on this topic. Remind students to tell the information in their own words and to list their sources.

Leveled Readers Use the Leveled Readers and Procedure Card 5 to build fluency and comprehension.

Name _____ Date _____

Part A

Vocabulary Words		Additional Words	
plantation	abolitionist	balance	conductor
slave state	secede	politician	emancipation
free state	civil war	runaway	
Underground Railroad			

Part B

1. Since colonial times, / enslaved Africans / had been forced to work in North America / on plantations.

2. As new states / were added to the United States, / Congress / tried to keep a balance / between free states and slave states.

3. Two Indiana politicians, / Stephen S. Harding and George W. Julian, / were well-known abolitionists.

4. The people who helped runaways / along the Underground Railroad / were known as conductors.

5. In 1861, / 11 Southern states / seceded from the United States / and formed their own government / called the Confederate States of America.

6. A battle / in 1861 / at Fort Sumter / in South Carolina / marked the start / of the American Civil War.

7. About 200,000 Hoosiers / served in the United States, / or Union, army / during the Civil War.

8. In 1863, / President Lincoln / issued the Emancipation Proclamation, / which gave freedom / to enslaved people / in the Confederate states.

YOU ARE THERE Turn to Student Edition page 150. Practice reading aloud "You Are There" three times. Try to improve your reading each time. Record your best time on the line below.

Number of words ___62___ My Best Time _____ Words per Minute _____

Name _____ Date _____

Lesson Title: _____

North and South

Southern states _____ Northern states _____

The Issue of Slavery   Effect on the nation _____

Indiana Abolitionists

The Underground Railroad   What it was _____

Who helped in Indiana _____

Anti-Slavery Groups   Why groups were formed _____

Colonization Movement   Country in Africa _____

The Civil War in Indiana

Hoosiers in the Civil War   When war started _____

Number of Hoosiers who served in the Union army _____

Morgan's Raid   Battle in Indiana _____

The Home Front   What women did _____

_____

An End to Slavery   When _____ President _____

What he issued _____ When the war ended _____

LESSON 3 Changes in Indiana

Vocabulary Strategies

Preteach Additional Vocabulary After teaching the Vocabulary words on Student Edition page 160, explain to students that there are several other important words they will see in this lesson. Use Procedure Card 1, along with the suggestions below, to introduce the words.

amendment	Tell students that an amendment is a change or improvement. Discuss why it is important to have a process for adding amendments to the United States Constitution.
ratify	Give *approve* as a synonym for *ratify*. Have students substitute *approved* for *ratified* in this sentence: "In December 1865, the Thirteenth Amendment to the Constitution was ratified."
technology	Discuss with students how technology, or the use of scientific knowledge and tools, has changed people's lives.
raw materials	Tell students that raw materials are resources that are used to make a product. Give examples, such as wood used to make a desk. Invite students to give additional examples.
natural gas	Have students name types of fuels. Explain that natural gas is gas that is formed beneath the earth's crust.

WORD CARDS To help teach the lesson vocabulary, use the Word Cards on pages 139–140.

Build Fluency

Use page 60 and the steps on Procedure Card 2 to reinforce vocabulary and build fluency. Read each vocabulary word aloud and have students repeat it. Then have students work in pairs to reread the words. Follow a similar procedure with the phrases and sentences. Continue to help students build fluency by having them reread "You Are There" in the Student Edition.

Text Comprehension

BEFORE READING

Preview the Lesson Guide students in previewing the lesson using Procedure Card 3. Point out the following features of the lesson on Student Edition pages 160–165.

• **Pages 160–161** Read aloud the "What to Know" question. Preview the time line and the photograph of a girl working in a cotton mill. On page 161, preview the images of the Reconstruction era. Discuss the reasons why many formerly enslaved people became sharecroppers during Reconstruction. Explain briefly what the Freedmen's Bureau was and what it did.

- **Pages 162–163** Have students examine the illustrated feature on Indiana industrialists. Discuss what the images and captions tell about the growth of industry in Indiana.
- **Pages 164–165** Preview the photographs of a police officer directing traffic and railroad workers on page 164. Have students read and discuss the Fast Fact. Preview the photograph of Indiana schoolchildren on page 165. Explain that many schools were built in Indiana after the Civil War. Then preview the Review questions.

DURING READING

Build Comprehension of Expository Text Present the graphic organizer on page 61. Have students preview the organizer by filling in the lesson title and comparing the three main heads in the organizer with the matching subheads in the Student Edition pages 160–165. Tell students that the section subheads provide additional help with identifying important information. Use Procedure Card 4, the Reading Check questions in *Indiana Social Studies*, and the directed reading suggestions below.

- **Page 160** After students have read "You Are There," ask whether they know any children today who work in cotton mills. Discuss why and how this situation might have changed since 1850.
- **Page 161** Have students read "Time of Reconstruction" and summarize verbally the information under each section subhead, "Constitutional Amendments" and "African Americans." Then have students write brief summaries in the boxes with these subheads in the graphic organizer.
- **Pages 162–163** After students have read "Industries Grow," have them summarize the information under each section subhead verbally and then write brief summaries in the boxes with the matching subheads.
- **Pages 164–165** Follow the same procedure used for the previous sections to have students read "Changes in Society" and complete the organizer.

AFTER READING

Summarize Have students use their completed graphic organizers to summarize the lesson. Then have them compare their summaries to the lesson summary on page 165.

Review and Respond Work through the Review questions with students. If students need additional help with summarizing, use Focus Skill Transparency 3.

Make a Chart Suggest that students reread the section of the lesson that tells about new industries that developed in Indiana. Tell them to jot down information they might want to include in their charts. Then discuss with students how they might construct their charts and what headings they might use. You may want to have students create their charts on a computer.

Leveled Readers Use the Leveled Readers and Procedure Card 5 to build fluency and comprehension.

Name _____ Date _____

Part A

Vocabulary Words		Additional Words	
Reconstruction	manufacturing	amendment	raw materials
sharecropping	refinery	ratify	natural gas
automobile	labor union	technology	

Part B

1. The Thirteenth Amendment to the Constitution, / which ended slavery in the United States, / was ratified / in December 1865.

2. During Reconstruction, / many formerly enslaved people / began sharecropping.

3. In the late 1800s, / new technologies / made farm work / easier and faster.

4. Elwood Haynes / invented / one of the first gasoline-powered automobiles / in 1894.

5. Indiana's natural resources / and its transportation systems / helped manufacturing grow / in the state.

6. In 1886, / natural gas / was discovered / in northern Indiana, / near Portland.

7. In 1889, / the Standard Oil Company / built one of the world's largest oil refineries / near Whiting.

8. To improve working conditions, / workers / formed labor unions.

9. Railroads / transported / raw materials to factories / and goods to markets.

YOU ARE THERE Turn to Student Edition page 160. Practice reading aloud "You Are There" three times. Try to improve your reading each time. Record your best time on the line below.

Number of words ___80___ My Best Time _____ Words per Minute _____

Lesson Title: _____

Time of Reconstruction

Constitutional Amendments

African Americans

Industries Grow

Changes in Agriculture

New Businesses

Manufacturing

Changes in Society

Labor Unions

Urban Centers

Education

LESSON 4 **A New Century**

Vocabulary Strategies

Preteach Additional Vocabulary After teaching the Vocabulary words on Student Edition page 166, explain to students that there are several other important words they will see in this lesson. Use Procedure Card 1, along with the suggestions below, to introduce the words.

supplies	Have students name types of supplies that soldiers might need, such as food, clothing, blankets, weapons, and so on.
submarine	Tell students that the word part *sub* is from Latin and often means "under" or "below." The word *marine* is from the Latin *mare*, which means "sea."
volunteer	Ask students to give examples of people who volunteer their time to help others, such as young people who help in hospitals or those who join organizations to build homes for people who need them.
public office	Tell students someone who holds public office has been elected to a position in government. Have students give examples of people in public office, such as mayors, senators, the President, and so on.
mechanization	Have students read this sentence: "The ways in which farmers planted and harvested crops became mechanized, or powered by machines." Write and compare *mechanized* and *mechanization*.

WORD CARDS To help teach the lesson vocabulary, use the Word Cards on pages 139–140.

Build Fluency

Use page 64 and the steps on Procedure Card 2 to reinforce vocabulary and build fluency. Read each vocabulary word aloud and have students repeat it. Then have students work in pairs to reread the words. Follow a similar procedure with the phrases and sentences. Continue to help students build fluency by having them reread "You Are There" in the Student Edition.

Text Comprehension

BEFORE READING

Preview the Lesson Guide students in previewing the lesson using Procedure Card 3. Point out the following features of the lesson on Student Edition pages 166–171.

• **Pages 166–167** Read aloud the "What to Know" question. Call attention to the time line, and ask whether students think these events affected Indiana. Preview the photograph of the farewell parade for World War I soldiers.

- **Pages 168–169** Preview the photograph on page 168. Tell students that thousands of African Americans moved from the South to cities in the North between 1910 and 1930. This movement of people became known as the Great Migration. Preview the photograph of suffragists in Indiana on page 169. Have students recall the meaning of *suffrage*. Explain that the Nineteenth Amendment gave women the right to vote.

- **Pages 170–171** Have students read and discuss the Primary Sources feature on the Indianapolis 500. Discuss the Document-Based Question. Then preview the photograph of a tractor and the Review questions on page 171.

DURING READING

Build Comprehension of Expository Text Present the graphic organizer on page 65. Have students preview the organizer by filling in the lesson title and comparing the four main heads in the organizer with the matching subheads in the Student Edition pages 166–171. Tell students that the section subheads provide additional help with identifying important information. Use Procedure Card 4, the Reading Check questions in *Indiana Social Studies*, and the directed reading suggestions below.

- **Page 166** After students have read "You Are There," discuss how a war so far away might have affected the lives of people in Indiana.

- **Pages 167–168** Have students read "World War I." Discuss briefly how the war affected Indiana. Then call attention to the structure of the graphic organizer for this section of the lesson. Guide students in locating the information and filling in this part of the organizer. Follow a similar procedure to have students read and write information about "The Great Migration" on page 168.

- **Pages 169–171** After students have read "Women Gain the Vote," discuss the information briefly. Then have students fill in the next part of the organizer. Remind them to use the two section subheads to locate information. Follow a similar procedure to have students read "Developments in Indiana" and complete the organizer.

AFTER READING

Summarize Have students use their completed graphic organizers to summarize the lesson. Then have them compare their summaries to the lesson summary on page 171.

Review and Respond Work through the Review questions with students. If students need additional help with summarizing, use Focus Skill Transparency 3.

Write a Diary Entry Encourage students to reread page 169 and jot down information they may want to use in their diary entries. Discuss the idea that a diary entry might give the point of view of someone who supported the Nineteenth Amendment or of someone who opposed it. Remind students to write in the first person and to express opinions and feelings as well as facts.

Leveled Readers Use the Leveled Readers and Procedure Card 5 to build fluency and comprehension.

Name _____ Date _____

Part A

Vocabulary Words		Additional Words	
bond	interurban rail	supplies	volunteer
suffrage	consumer goods	submarine	public office
		mechanization	

Part B

1. When World War I / broke out in Europe, / the United States / sent supplies / to support the Allies.

2. After German submarines / attacked United States ships, / the United States Congress / declared war on Germany.

3. Women / went to work in factories, / volunteered with the Red Cross, / and served in the military / as nurses.

4. Many Hoosiers / bought war bonds.

5. In the early 1900s, / women were still not allowed / to hold public office / or vote.

6. By 1890, / about 100,000 women in Indiana / had joined groups / that worked for woman's suffrage / and other rights.

7. The interurban rail system / connected rural areas / with nearby cities.

8. When World War I ended, / factories / switched from making war supplies / to making consumer goods.

9. Mechanization / allowed farms / to produce more crops / with fewer workers.

YOU ARE THERE Turn to Student Edition page 166. Practice reading aloud "You Are There" three times. Try to improve your reading each time. Record your best time on the line below.

Number of words ___73___ My Best Time _____ Words per Minute _____

Name _____ Date _____

Lesson Title: _____

World War I

When it began _____ When the United States declared war _____

Hoosiers Go to War How many
went from Indiana _____

On the Home Front Who helped
_____

The Great Migration

When _____ What happened _____

Facing Challenges How African
Americans were treated _____

Overcoming Challenges How
_____
_____
_____

Women Gain the Vote

Banding Together Worked for
_____

The Nineteenth Amendment When
_____

Developments in Indiana

Transportation Inventions that made
travel easier _____
_____

Industry Factories switched to
_____

What changed farming _____

Unit 3

Challenging Times

Vocabulary Strategies

Preteach Additional Vocabulary After teaching the Vocabulary words on Student Edition page 174, explain to students that there are several other important words they will see in this lesson. Use Procedure Card 1, along with the suggestions below, to introduce the words.

value	Tell students that the word *value* has several different meanings. Sometimes we express the value of something by the amount of money it is worth.
worthless	Point out the familiar word *worth* and suffix *-less*. Explain that the suffix *-less* means "without," as in *hopeless* and *fearless*. Something that is worthless has no value.
repay	Have students identify the base word *pay* and prefix *re-*. Have two students role play a scene in which one borrows money from the other. Then have them role play the borrower repaying the loan.
program	Discuss meanings that students know for this word. Then discuss the meaning in this context: "Under this plan, the government set up programs to give people jobs."
scrap	Ask a volunteer to hold up a scrap of paper. Explain that scrap is material that is usually thrown away. Ask students what scrap metal is and where they might find scrap metal.

WORD CARDS To help teach the lesson vocabulary, use the Word Cards on pages 139–142.

Build Fluency

Use page 68 and the steps on Procedure Card 2 to reinforce vocabulary and build fluency. Read each vocabulary word aloud and have students repeat it. Then have students work in pairs to reread the words. Follow a similar procedure with the phrases and sentences. Continue to help students build fluency by having them reread "You Are There" in the Student Edition.

Text Comprehension

BEFORE READING

Preview the Lesson Guide students in previewing the lesson using Procedure Card 3. Point out the following features of the lesson on Student Edition pages 174–179.

- **Pages 174–175** Read aloud the "What to Know" question. Point out that challenging times might also be called difficult times. Preview the time line and the photograph of people standing in line for bread during the Great Depression. Have students read and discuss the Fast Fact.

- **Pages 176–177** Preview the photographs of the New Deal on page 176. Tell students that President Roosevelt's New Deal programs helped people find jobs, such as building roads or painting murals on the walls of public buildings. Preview the photographs of the Evansville Shipyard and welder Evelyn Cox on page 177.

- **Pages 178–179** Preview the photograph on page 178, and explain briefly the system of ration coupons. Then preview the Review questions. Call attention to the biography of Ernie Pyle on page 179. Tell students that Pyle was a well-known newspaper columnist during World War II.

DURING READING

Build Comprehension of Expository Text Present the graphic organizer on page 69. Have students preview the organizer by filling in the lesson title and comparing the three main heads in the organizer with the matching subheads in the Student Edition pages 174–178. Tell students that the section subheads provide additional help with identifying important information. Use Procedure Card 4, the Reading Check questions in *Indiana Social Studies*, and the directed reading suggestions below.

- **Page 174** After students have read "You Are There," ask what they think may happen to this family if times do not get better soon.

- **Page 175** Before students read "The Great Depression," point out that the graphic organizer is a sequence diagram. Have students use the organizer to set a purpose for reading. Then point out that the subhead in the second box matches the section subhead in the text. Students may want to read up to that subhead, then pause and fill in the first box before going back to the text to read "The Stock Market Crash" and filling in the second box.

- **Pages 176–178** Follow a similar procedure to have students set a purpose and read "The Government Helps" and fill in the next two boxes in the organizer. Do the same to have students read "World War II" and complete the organizer. Then have students review the dates they have written in the organizer to confirm that these dates are in correct time order.

AFTER READING

Summarize Have students use their completed graphic organizers to summarize the lesson. Then have them compare their summaries to the lesson summary on page 178.

Review and Respond Work through the Review questions with students. If students need additional help with summarizing, use Focus Skill Transparency 3.

Make an Illustrated Time Line You may want to have students work in pairs or small groups to construct and illustrate time lines. Point out that students can use their completed graphic organizers, as well as information and illustrations in their texts, as a source of ideas. Have students use their completed time lines to create a classroom display.

Leveled Readers Use the Leveled Readers and Procedure Card 5 to build fluency and comprehension.

Name _____ Date _____

Part A

Vocabulary Words		Additional Words	
stock	shortage	value	program
depression	rationing	worthless	scrap
unemployed	recycle	repay	

Part B

1. The fast growth of businesses / in the 1920s / made stocks / go up
   in value.

2. In October 1929, / stock prices / began to fall, / and most stocks / became
   worthless.

3. The stock market crash of 1929 / helped lead / to a severe depression.

4. People / could not repay the money / they had borrowed from banks, /
   so most banks / were forced to close.

5. By 1933, / one out of four Hoosiers / was unemployed.

6. Under a plan / called the New Deal, / the government / set up programs /
   to give people jobs.

7. The needs of the armed forces / created shortages of meat, / sugar, /
   and gasoline/ during World War II.

8. To make sure / that soldiers had enough, / the government / called for
   rationing.

9. Many people / collected scrap metal/ old tires, / and paper / to be
   recycled.

YOU ARE THERE Turn to Student Edition page 174. Practice reading aloud "You Are There" three
times. Try to improve your reading each time. Record your best time on the
line below.

Number of words ___74___   My Best Time _____   Words per Minute _____

Name _____ Date _____

Lesson Title: _____

BREAD LINE ↓

The Great Depression

When _____ What happened _____

_____

⬇

The Stock Market Crash When _____ Effects of crash _____

_____

⬇

The Government Helps

What happened to businesses _____

_____

⬇

A Plan for the Nation When _____ New President _____

Plan _____ What it did _____

⬇

World War II

When war began _____ Date of Pearl Harbor attack _____

⬇

Indiana Lends a Hand How _____

⬇

Hoosiers at Home How they helped _____

_____ When war ended _____

LESSON 6 **Into Modern Times**

Vocabulary Strategies

Preteach Additional Vocabulary After teaching the Vocabulary words on Student Edition page 180, explain to students that there are several other important words they will see in this lesson. Use Procedure Card 1, along with the suggestions below, to introduce the words.

access	Define access as "the ability to enter or to pass to and from." On a map, show how ships leaving the Port of Indiana on Lake Michigan have access to the Atlantic Ocean.
seaway	Have students identify the two shorter words that make up this compound word. Point out the St. Lawrence Seaway on a map, and have students tell why it is called a seaway.
invade	Discuss what happens when an army invades. Draw a simple picture or diagram to help students understand that an army that invades comes into an area that belongs to the other side.
republic	Tell students that a republic is a form of government in which people elect representatives to govern the country. Challenge students to recall how *republic* is used in the Pledge of Allegiance.
protest	Discuss actions that Americans can take to protest something they do not like. (write letters, make speeches, hold marches or demonstrations, and so on)

WORD CARDS To help teach the lesson vocabulary, use the Word Cards on pages 141–142.

Build Fluency

Use page 72 and the steps on Procedure Card 2 to reinforce vocabulary and build fluency. Read each vocabulary word aloud and have students repeat it. Then have students work in pairs to reread the words. Follow a similar procedure with the phrases and sentences. Continue to help students build fluency by having them reread "You Are There" in the Student Edition.

Text Comprehension

BEFORE READING

Preview the Lesson Guide students in previewing the lesson using Procedure Card 3. Point out the following features of the lesson on Student Edition pages 180–185.

- **Pages 180–181** Read aloud the "What to Know" question. Preview the time line and the photographs of life after World War II. Discuss how life for the people in these photographs seems different from people's lives during the Great Depression and World War II.

- **Pages 182–183** Have students examine the map of Korea and the photograph of the Korean War Memorial on page 182. Discuss the map skill question. Then have students examine the map of Vietnam and the photograph on page 183 and answer the map skill question.

- **Pages 184–185** Preview the photograph of a civil rights march in Indianapolis. Have students recall the meaning of civil rights and discuss the reasons that civil rights are so important. Then preview the photograph of a business owner and the Review questions on page 185.

DURING READING

Build Comprehension of Expository Text Present the graphic organizer on page 73. Have students preview the organizer by filling in the lesson title and comparing the five main heads in the organizer with the matching subheads in the Student Edition pages 180–185. Tell students that the section subheads provide additional help with identifying important information. Use Procedure Card 4, the Reading Check questions in *Indiana Social Studies*, and the directed reading suggestions below.

- **Page 180** After students have read "You Are There," invite them to compare the car in the photograph with today's cars.

- **Page 181** Have students read "Growth After World War II." Tell them to list in the graphic organizer some important changes they read about in this section of the lesson.

- **Page 182** After students have read "The Korean War," have them fill in the box for this section in the graphic organizer. Point out that some information that students need for the organizer is found in the text before the section subhead. Under the subhead "North and South Korea," students will write a brief summary to tell what happened.

- **Pages 183–185** Have students read and discuss "The Vietnam War" and fill in the next box in the organizer. Then have students read "Civil Rights" and fill in that box. After students have read the last section of the lesson, "Immigration," tell them to list in the last box some changes that took place in Indiana because of immigration between 1970 and today.

AFTER READING

Summarize Have students use their completed graphic organizers to summarize the lesson. Then have them compare their summaries to the lesson summary on page 185.

Review and Respond Work through the Review questions with students. If students need additional help with summarizing, use Focus Skill Transparency 3.

Write Newspaper Headlines You may want to provide several examples of newspaper headlines. Discuss briefly how headlines are worded to give important information in just a few words. Suggest that students reread the section of the lesson about the Korean War.

Leveled Readers Use the Leveled Readers and Procedure Card 5 to build fluency and comprehension.

Name _____ Date _____

Read aloud the words in Part A. Practice reading aloud the
phrases and the sentences in Part B.

Part A

Vocabulary Words		Additional Words	
communism	civil rights	access	republic
cold war	discrimination	seaway	protest
cease-fire	segregation	invade	

Part B

1. The Port of Indiana / on Lake Michigan / has access to the Atlantic
   Ocean / through the St. Lawrence Seaway.

2. The conflict / between the United States / and the Soviet Union /
   over communism / became known as the Cold War.

3. On June 25, 1950, / North Korean soldiers / invaded South Korea.

4. In 1953, / both sides / agreed to a cease-fire, / and the war ended.

5. In the late 1950s, / North Vietnam / had a communist government, /
   and South Vietnam / was a republic.

6. Hoosiers who were upset / by the loss of life / in the Vietnam War /
   took to the streets / to protest.

7. Many African Americans / and white people / in the United States /
   joined the Civil Rights movement.

8. African Americans / often faced discrimination / because of their race.

9. In 1949, / the Indiana General Assembly / made segregation in schools /
   illegal.

You ARE THERE Turn to Student Edition page 180. Practice reading aloud "You Are There"
three times. Try to improve your reading each time. Record your best time on
the line below.

Number of words ___70___ My Best Time _____ Words per Minute _____

Lesson Title: _____

Growth After World War II

A Changing State   Changes

_____

_____

_____

The Korean War

Conflict with communism _____

North and South Korea

What happened _____

_____

_____

_____

The Vietnam War

The United States Sends Soldiers

What happened _____

_____

_____

_____

Divided Support   Why _____

_____

Civil Rights

Working for Equality   What

workers wanted _____

_____

Changes _____

_____

_____

Immigration

Changes in Indiana _____

_____

_____

_____

_____

_____

LESSON 7 Recent Times

Vocabulary Strategies

Preteach Additional Vocabulary After teaching the Vocabulary words on Student Edition page 188, explain to students that there are several other important words they will see in this lesson. Use Procedure Card 1, along with the suggestions below, to introduce the words.

terrorist	Write *terrorism* and *terrorist* and have students compare the two words. Remind students that words with the suffix *-ism* often refer to ideas or beliefs, while words with the suffix *-ist* refer to people.
Pentagon	Draw and identify a pentagon. Explain that its name is from the Greek word *penta*, meaning "five." The headquarters of the Department of Defense in Washington, D. C., called the Pentagon, is this shape.
counter-terrorism	Ask students to demonstrate the difference between clockwise and counterclockwise movements. Then ask them to define *counter-terrorism*.
updated	Have students identify the two shorter words that make up this compound word. Discuss this sentence: "The companies could afford new and updated farming equipment."
key	Point out that we often use *key* as a noun. However, it is also used as an adjective. Synonyms include *important* and *basic*.

WORD CARDS To help teach the lesson vocabulary, use the Word Cards on pages 141–144.

Build Fluency

Use page 76 and the steps on Procedure Card 2 to reinforce vocabulary and build fluency. Read each vocabulary word aloud and have students repeat it. Then have students work in pairs to reread the words. Follow a similar procedure with the phrases and sentences. Continue to help students build fluency by having them reread "You Are There" in the Student Edition.

Text Comprehension

BEFORE READING

Preview the Lesson Guide students in previewing the lesson using Procedure Card 3. Point out the following features of the lesson on Student Edition pages 188–193.

• **Pages 188–189** Read aloud the "What to Know" question. Preview the time line and the photograph of the space shuttle *Endeavour* on page 188. Invite students to share briefly any information they know about space shuttles. Then preview the photographs on page 189.

- **Pages 190–191** Preview the photograph of the Farm Aid concert on page 190 and the photographs of Indiana workers on page 191. Explain that students will read about changes to Indiana's economy.

- **Pages 192–193** Have students recall the meaning of *high-tech*. Preview the photograph of a worker in a high-tech industry on page 192 and the photograph of astronaut Gus Grissom, born in Indiana, on page 193. Then preview the Review questions.

DURING READING

Build Comprehension of Expository Text Present the graphic organizer on page 77. Have students preview the organizer by filling in the lesson title and comparing the three main heads in the organizer with the matching subheads in the Student Edition pages 188-193. Tell students that the section subheads provide additional help with identifying important information. Use Procedure Card 4, the Reading Check questions in *Indiana Social Studies*, and the directed reading suggestions below.

- **Page 188** After students have read "You Are There," ask whether they would like to be astronauts like Janice Voss, and why or why not.

- **Page 189** After reading "Facing New Dangers," have students identify and write the new danger in the first box of the graphic organizer. Guide students in making an oral summary of the information under the section subhead "A New Threat." Then have them write a brief summary in the organizer.

- **Pages 190–191** For the next section of the lesson, "Businesses Change," have students first summarize orally the information under the section subhead "Farmers Struggle" and then write a brief summary in the organizer. Follow the same procedure for each of the other section subheads.

- **Pages 192–193** Have students read "High Technology in Indiana," summarize orally the information under each section subhead, and then write brief summaries to complete the organizer.

AFTER READING

Summarize Have students use their completed graphic organizers to summarize the lesson. Then have them compare their summaries to the lesson summary on page 193.

Review and Respond Work through the Review questions with students. If students need additional help with summarizing, use Focus Skill Transparency 3.

Write an Essay Have students identify and reread parts of the lesson that give information about how industries in Indiana have changed. Suggest that students make notes as they read. Remind them to begin with a topic sentence and to write their essays in own words.

Leveled Readers Use the Leveled Readers and Procedure Card 5 to build fluency and comprehension.

Name _____ Date _____

Read aloud the words in Part A. Practice reading aloud the phrases and the sentences in Part B.

Part A

Vocabulary Words		Additional Words	
terrorism	high-tech	terrorist	updated
efficient	aerospace	Pentagon	key
service industry		counter-terrorism	

Part B

1. At home, / the United States / faced a new danger — / terrorism.

2. On September 11, 2001, / terrorists / flew two planes / into the World Trade Center / in New York City.

3. A third plane / hit the Pentagon / in Washington, D.C.

4. Indiana governor Frank O'Bannon / created / the Counter-Terrorism and Security Council.

5. In the 1960s, / new and updated farming equipment / helped farmers in Indiana / raise more crops / using fewer workers.

6. Even though / some of Indiana's factories closed, / manufacturing / remained key / to Indiana's economy.

7. New technology / has helped factories / be efficient.

8. Indiana's service industries / began to grow rapidly / in the 1980s and 1990s.

9. Several high-tech companies / make medical products / in Indiana.

10. About 100 aerospace companies / are located in Indiana.

YOU ARE THERE Turn to Student Edition page 188. Practice reading aloud "You Are There" three times. Try to improve your reading each time. Record your best time on the line below.

Number of words ___75___ My Best Time _____ Words per Minute _____

Name _____ Date _____

Lesson Title: _____

Facing New Dangers

A New Threat The new danger _____ Summary _____

_____

_____

Businesses Change

Farmers Struggle Summary _____

_____

Industries Struggle Summary _____

_____

Hoosiers Adapt to Change Summary _____

_____

High Technology in Indiana

High-Tech Industries Summary _____

_____

_____

Indiana and Aerospace Summary _____

_____

_____

_____

LESSON 1 # Indiana Industries

Vocabulary Strategies

Preteach Additional Vocabulary After teaching the Vocabulary words on Student Edition page 212, explain to students that there are several other important words they will see in this lesson. Use Procedure Card 1, along with the suggestions below, to introduce the words.

diverse	Give *varied* and *mixed* as synonyms for *diverse*. Discuss the concept of a diverse economy.
billion	Write 1,000,000,000 and challenge students to identify this number. (*one billion*) Ask how many millions there are in one billion. (*one thousand*)
ground	Have students give familiar meanings for this word. Point out that *ground* is also the past tense of *grind*. Challenge students to change this sentence from present tense to past tense: "Mills grind corn into flour."
process	Explain that this word has several different meanings. When foods are processed, they are changed in some way, such as by cooking, canning, freezing, adding other ingredients, and so on.
timber	Ask what it means when a logger or lumberjack calls out, "Timber!" Tell students that growing trees or their wood is called timber.

WORD CARDS To help teach the lesson vocabulary, use the Word Cards on pages 145–146.

Build Fluency

Use page 80 and the steps on Procedure Card 2 to reinforce vocabulary and build fluency. Read each vocabulary word aloud and have students repeat it. Then have students work in pairs to reread the words. Follow a similar procedure with the phrases and sentences. Continue to help students build fluency by having them reread "You Are There" in the Student Edition.

Text Comprehension

BEFORE READING

Preview the Lesson Guide students in previewing the lesson using Procedure Card 3. Point out the following features of the lesson on Student Edition pages 212–217.

- **Pages 212–213** Read aloud the "What to Know" question. Preview the photographs and the Food Production graph. Have students answer the question in the caption. Then ask students what they have learned from their preview so far that may help them answer the "What to Know" question.

- **Pages 214–215** Have students recall the meaning of *productivity*. Then have them examine and discuss the illustrated time line, Productivity in Indiana.

- **Pages 216–217** Preview the map of Indiana Manufactured Products on page 216, and have students use the map key to answer the map skill question. Then preview the photograph of a researcher and the Review questions on page 217.

DURING READING

Build Comprehension of Expository Text Present the graphic organizer on page 81. Have students preview the organizer by filling in the lesson title and comparing the three main heads in the organizer with the matching subheads in the Student Edition pages 212–217. Tell students that the section subheads provide additional help with identifying important information. Use Procedure Card 4, the Reading Check questions in *Indiana Social Studies*, and the directed reading suggestions below.

- **Page 212** After students have read "You Are There," invite them to tell what jobs they might like to have one day and how they think they might prepare for those jobs.

- **Page 213** Have students read "Indiana's Economy." Guide them in identifying and writing in the first box of the graphic organizer a one-word description of Indiana's economy. Then have students write information in the two boxes with subheads that match the section subheads in the text.

- **Pages 214–215** After students have read "A Changing Economy," guide them in identifying and writing the information in the appropriate box. Point out that the subheads in the three following boxes match the section subheads in the text. Students can use the subheads to locate the information and fill in these boxes.

- **Pages 216–217** Have students read "The Economy Today." Discuss what they have learned about Indiana's diverse economy today. Then have them complete the organizer. Again, point out the four subheads that match the section subheads.

AFTER READING

Summarize Have students use their completed graphic organizers to summarize the lesson. Then have them compare their summaries to the lesson summary on page 217.

Review and Respond Work through the Review questions with students. Use Focus Skill Transparency 4, Compare and Contrast, to guide students in making comparisons and contrasts based on information in the lesson.

Write a Job Description Tell students that your job is being a teacher. Invite them to describe a teacher's job and some of the duties they think it involves. Jot notes on the board as students speak. Then tell them to think about jobs they know about or might like to have. Students can then make their own notes and use the notes to write their paragraphs.

Leveled Readers Use the Leveled Readers and Procedure Card 5 to build fluency and comprehension.

Name _____ Date _____

Part A

Vocabulary Words		Additional Words	
economy	competition	billion	timber
productivity	ethanol	chemicals	diverse
surplus	tourism	process	
gross state product			

Part B

1. Indiana / has a diverse economy.

2. Indiana's GSP, / or gross state product, / in 2006 / was about $215 billion.

3. The productivity of agriculture / has increased dramatically / over the years.

4. Focusing on growing corn / and raising hogs / allowed farmers / to produce a surplus.

5. Mills that ground corn into flour / and factories that processed pork / were centers of activity.

6. During the late 1800s, / industries / used more of the state's resources, / including its timber, / coal, / and oil.

7. In the 1970s and 1980s, / Indiana factories / began to face more competition / from factories in other places.

8. Today, / Indiana's economy / has become more diverse.

9. Some corn / grown in Indiana / is made into ethanol.

10. Tourism / is a growing service industry / in Indiana.

YOU ARE THERE Turn to Student Edition page 212. Practice reading aloud "You Are There" three times. Try to improve your reading each time. Record your best time on the line below.

Number of words ___75___   My Best Time _____   Words per Minute _____

Name _____ Date _____

Lesson Title: _____

Indiana's Economy

Type of economy _____

The Gross State Product In 2006
_____

Productivity Change in agriculture
_____

A Changing Economy

Changed from mostly _____

to mostly _____

The Economy Develops Two important services _____

Growth Continues What towns needed _____

New Industries What businesses added _____

The Economy Today

Economy has become _____

Agriculture and Mining How most

work is done _____

Manufacturing Who factories employ
_____

Service Industries Who they employ
_____

Life Sciences What the industry

has done _____

LESSON 2 Indiana's Entrepreneurs

Vocabulary Strategies

Preteach Additional Vocabulary After teaching the Vocabulary words on Student Edition page 222, explain to students that there are several other important words they will see in this lesson. Use Procedure Card 1, along with the suggestions below, to introduce the words.

risky	Point out the root word *risk* with the suffix *-y* added to form an adjective. Have students give examples of other words in which *-y* is added to a noun to form an adjective. (*rainy, cloudy, rocky*)
expenses	Tell students that expenses are money that is paid or spent. Discuss the kinds of expenses that a business might have, such as rent for a building, employees' salaries, electricity, and so on.
corporation	Give *business* and *company* as synonyms for *corporation*.
diesel	Tell students that this word is an example of a word that was originally a person's name. The diesel engine is named for Rudolf Diesel, a German mechanical engineer,
global	Explain that this adjective is formed from the noun *globe* by adding the suffix *-al*, meaning "of, relating to." The word *global* describes things that relate to all of Earth.

WORD CARDS To help teach the lesson vocabulary, use the Word Cards on pages 145–146.

Build Fluency

Use page 84 and the steps on Procedure Card 2 to reinforce vocabulary and build fluency. Read each vocabulary word aloud and have students repeat it. Then have students work in pairs to reread the words. Follow a similar procedure with the phrases and sentences. Continue to help students build fluency by having them reread "You Are There" in the Student Edition.

BEFORE READING

Preview the Lesson Guide students in previewing the lesson using Procedure Card 3. Point out the following features of the lesson on Student Edition pages 222–227.

• **Pages 222–223** Read aloud the "What to Know" question. Preview the photograph of a farmers' market. Have students examine the illustrated chart "Starting a Business" and explain it in their own words. Then have them answer the question in the caption.

• **Pages 224–225** Have students examine the photographs of early entrepreneurs in Indiana and discuss the information in the captions.

• **Pages 226–227** Preview the photograph on page 226. Tell students that the Griffiths are an example of Indiana entrepreneurs today. Preview the Review questions. Then call attention to the biography of entrepreneur William G. Mays, founder of Mays Chemical Company, on page 227.

Build Comprehension of Expository Text Present the graphic organizer on page 85. Have students preview the organizer by filling in the lesson title and comparing the three main heads in the organizer with the matching subheads in the Student Edition pages 222–226. Tell students that the section subheads provide additional help with identifying important information. Use Procedure Card 4, the Reading Check questions in *Indiana Social Studies*, and the directed reading suggestions below.

- **Page 222** After students have read "You Are There," have them identify the reasons that the farmers' market may succeed. Then have students suggest reasons that the business might fail. For example, the prices may be too high, customers may prefer the convenience of shopping at a supermarket, and so on.

- **Page 223** Have students read and discuss "Entrepreneurs." Then have them fill in the first box in the graphic organizer. Remind them to use the section subhead "Risk and Profit" to help them locate the information.

- **Pages 224–225** Tell students that they can fill in the chart on the graphic organizer either as they read or after reading the next section of the lesson, "Early Entrepreneurs." Point out that the section subheads are the names of the early entrepreneurs that students will record in the chart.

- **Page 226** After students have read "Entrepreneurs Today," You may want to name additional entrepreneurs or businesses started by entrepreneurs in your community. Then have students complete the last box of the graphic organizer.

Summarize Have students use their completed graphic organizers to summarize the lesson. Then have them compare their summaries to the lesson summary on page 226.

Review and Respond Work through the Review questions with students. If students need additional help comparing and contrasting, use Focus Skill Transparency 4.

Create a Hall of Fame Point out that portraits of some entrepreneurs from the past and information about them can be found on pages 224 and 225. Discuss how students might find pictures of other entrepreneurs in reference books or on the Internet. Have students work in small groups to combine their drawings and captions to create a Hall of Fame classroom display.

Leveled Readers Use the Leveled Readers and Procedure Card 5 to build fluency and comprehension.

Name _____ Date _____

DIRECTIONS Read aloud the words in Part A. Practice reading aloud the phrases and the sentences in Part B.

Part A

Vocabulary Words	Additional Words	
entrepreneur	risky	diesel
profit	expenses	global
investor	corporation	

Part B

1. Throughout Indiana's history, / new businesses / have been started / by entrepreneurs.

2. Being an entrepreneur / can be risky / because many new businesses / fail.

3. However, / some do quite well / and can bring / a great deal of profit / to business owners.

4. Profit / is the money / that is left over / after all a business's expenses / have been paid.

5. Famous entrepreneurs of the past / include Eli Lilly, / the Ball brothers, / the Studebaker brothers, / and Madame C. J. Walker.

6. As an inventor, / Clessie Lyle Cummins / developed diesel engines.

7. In 1919, / Cummins founded / the Cummins Engine Company / with the help of an investor.

8. Indiana's businesses today / range from small neighborhood stores / to giant global corporations.

9. Entrepreneurs / continue to help Indiana's economy / grow.

YOU ARE THERE Turn to Student Edition page 222. Practice reading aloud "You Are There" three times. Try to improve your reading each time. Record your best time on the line below.

Number of words ____91____   My Best Time _____   Words per Minute _____

Lesson Title: _____

Entrepreneurs

Risk and Profit   Why entrepreneurs take the risk to start new businesses

_____

Early Entrepreneurs

Famous Entrepreneurs	Businesses and Products

Entrepreneurs Today

How many businesses in Indiana today _____

Effect of entrepreneurs on the state's economy _____

LESSON 3 **Trade in Indiana**

Vocabulary Strategies

Preteach Additional Vocabulary After teaching the Vocabulary words on Student Edition page 230, explain to students that there are several other important words they will see in this lesson. Use Procedure Card 1, along with the suggestions below, to introduce the words.

increase	Draw several short lines on the board. Then hand the chalk to a student and ask the student to increase the number of lines.
decrease	Now hand a student an eraser and ask that student to decrease the number of lines. Point out that *increase* and *decrease* are antonyms.
benefit	Explain that something that benefits someone helps that person. The word *benefit* is from the Latin *bene facere*, which means "to do good to."
interstate	Point out the prefix *inter-* and base word *state*. Remind students that the prefix *inter-* means "between." Ask students why they think some roads are called interstate highways.
international	Students can use the meaning of the prefix *inter-* in *interdependence* and *interstate* to determine the meaning of *international*. Ask what international companies do.

WORD CARDS To help teach the lesson vocabulary, use the Word Cards on pages 145–148.

Build Fluency

Use page 88 and the steps on Procedure Card 2 to reinforce vocabulary and build fluency. Read each vocabulary word aloud and have students repeat it. Then have students work in pairs to reread the words. Follow a similar procedure with the phrases and sentences. Continue to help students build fluency by having them reread "You Are There" in the Student Edition.

BEFORE READING

Preview the Lesson Guide students in previewing the lesson using Procedure Card 3. Point out the following features of the lesson on Student Edition pages 230–235.

- **Pages 230–231** Read aloud the "What to Know" question. Preview the photograph of the Port of Indiana-Jeffersonville on page 230 and the photograph of the family buying a new car on page 231. Have students examine the Supply and Demand chart. Encourage them to explain the diagram in their own words and then answer the question in the caption.

- **Pages 232–233** Preview the photographs of modern transportation. After reading aloud the captions, have students discuss briefly how these transportation methods help people trade within Indiana and with other states.

- **Pages 234–235** Have students examine the illustration of Indiana exports and the chart of Indiana's Top Export Markets in 2006. Discuss the question in the caption. Encourage students to challenge each other with additional questions based on the chart. Preview the Review questions on page 235.

Build Comprehension of Expository Text Present the graphic organizer on page 89. Have students preview the organizer by filling in the lesson title and comparing the four main heads in the organizer with the matching subheads in the Student Edition pages 230–235. Tell students that the section subheads provide additional help with identifying important information. Use Procedure Card 4, the Reading Check questions in *Indiana Social Studies,* and the directed reading suggestions below.

- **Page 230** After students have read "You Are There," ask whether they would like to work at the port and why or why not.

- **Page 231** Have students read "Supply and Demand." Ask them to explain in their own words how supply and demand affect prices. Discuss how and why competition affects prices. Then students can complete the two sentences in the first box of the graphic organizer.

- **Pages 232–233** After students have read "Trading Within Indiana," have them fill in the next box of the organizer. Remind them to use the two section subheads to help them locate information. Then have students read "Trading with Other States" and use the two section subheads to help them fill in the third box in the organizer.

- **Pages 234–235** Have students read "Trading with the World" and discuss the meaning and importance of global trade. Then have them complete the organizer. Point out the two subheads that match the section subheads in the text.

AFTER READING

Summarize Have students use their completed graphic organizers to summarize the lesson. Then have them compare their summaries to the lesson summary on page 235.

Review and Respond Work through the Review questions with students. If students need additional help comparing and contrasting, use Focus Skill Transparency 4.

Write a Summary Review briefly with students how to summarize. Suggest that they begin by rereading sections of the lesson and jotting down the most important information. At this point, you may want to have students compare their notes with a classmate. Partners should discuss why they have or have not included certain information. Then students can write their summaries individually. Remind them to write their summaries in their own words.

Leveled Readers Use the Leveled Readers and Procedure Card 5 to build fluency and comprehension.

Name _____ Date _____

Part A

Vocabulary Words		Additional Words	
supply	export	increase	interstate
demand	import	decrease	international
interdependence		benefit	

Part B

1. Business owners / think about supply and demand / when deciding what to make / and what to sell.

2. When the demand for a product / increases, / the price / will increase.

3. In contrast, / the price / will decrease / when the demand decreases.

4. When people / buy and sell / products and services, / both sides of the exchange / can benefit.

5. Indiana's trade with neighboring states / takes place mainly by interstate highways, / railroads, / and the St. Lawrence Seaway.

6. Trade / creates interdependence / between states in the Midwest.

7. The United States / sells many exports / around the world.

8. A country / that has just one major export / must then depend on imports / from other countries / for almost everything else.

9. More international companies / are coming to Indiana.

YOU ARE THERE Turn to Student Edition page 230. Practice reading aloud "You Are There" three times. Try to improve your reading each time. Record your best time on the line below.

Number of words ___94___ My Best Time _____ Words per Minute _____

Name _____ Date _____

Lesson Title: _____

Supply and Demand

Prices Change

When demand for a product increases, the price will _____ .

When the supply of a product increases, the price will _____ .

Trading Within Indiana

Trade in the Past   Where _____

Trade Today   How people move products _____

Trading with Other States

Trading with the Midwest   Biggest trading partners _____

_____

Interdependence   What people depend on people in other places for _____

_____

Trading with the World

World Trade What countries exchange

_____

_____

Indiana's Global Connections
Number of countries Indiana businesses
trade with _____

LESSON 4 **Indiana's State Government**

Vocabulary Strategies

Preteach Additional Vocabulary After teaching the Vocabulary words on Student Edition page 240, explain to students that there are several other important words they will see in this lesson. Use Procedure Card 1, along with the suggestions below, to introduce the words.

article	Have students give familiar meanings for this word. Explain that a document such as a constitution may be divided into separate parts. Each part is called an article.
yearly	Point out the base word *year* and suffix *-ly*. Explain that an event that takes place yearly happens once a year. Ask how often events happen that take place monthly, weekly, and daily.
approve	Have students read this sentence: "The governor can either approve or veto, or reject, bills the legislature passes." Point out that *veto* and *reject* are synonyms. The word *approve* is an antonym of *veto* and *reject*.
court	Tell students that this word has more than one meaning. A building where trials are held is called a court. However, *court* also refers to the events that take place there. Students may know other meanings, such as a basketball court or tennis court.
official	Ask students to give examples of government officials. (Possible responses: mayor, governor, senator.)

WORD CARDS To help teach the lesson vocabulary, use the Word Cards on pages 147–148.

Build Fluency

Use page 92 and the steps on Procedure Card 2 to reinforce vocabulary and build fluency. Read each vocabulary word aloud and have students repeat it. Then have students work in pairs to reread the words. Follow a similar procedure with the phrases and sentences. Continue to help students build fluency by having them reread "You Are There" in the Student Edition.

BEFORE READING

Preview the Lesson Guide students in previewing the lesson using Procedure Card 3. Point out the following features of the lesson on Student Edition pages 240–245.

- **Pages 240–241** Read aloud the "What to Know" question. Have students recall the three Vocabulary words for this lesson that name branches of government. Then have students examine the illustration of the Indiana Statehouse and answer the question in the caption.

- **Pages 242–243** Preview the photograph of the Indiana Government Center on page 242, and have students identify the rotunda of the Indiana Statehouse in this photograph. Then students can examine the illustrated table of the branches of Indiana's state government on page 243 and answer the question in the caption.

• **Pages 244–245** Preview the photographs of Indiana government officials on page 244. On page 245, preview the photograph of Chief Justice John Roberts. Then preview the Review questions.

Build Comprehension of Expository Text Present the graphic organizer on page 93. Have students preview the organizer by filling in the lesson title and comparing the four main heads in the organizer with the matching subheads in the Student Edition pages 240–245. Tell students that the section subheads provide additional help with identifying important information. Use Procedure Card 4, the Reading Check questions in *Indiana Social Studies,* and the directed reading suggestions below.

• **Page 240** After students have read "You Are There," have them point out on the illustration on pages 240-241 each place the class visits on the Statehouse tour.

• **Page 241** Have students read and discuss "Indiana's Constitution." Then have them fill in the first box in the graphic organizer. Point out the placement of the subhead "Bill of Rights," which matches the section subhead in the text.

• **Pages 242–243** After students have read "Branches of Government," have them name the three branches and briefly describe each branch. Then have students fill in the next part of the organizer. Point out that the subheads for the three smaller boxes name the three branches of government and match the section subheads in the text.

• **Pages 244–245** Have students read "State Leaders" and fill in the corresponding box in the organizer. Tell them to write the names of the offices, not the names of the people who currently hold those offices. Then students can read and discuss "The Federal System" and complete the organizer.

Summarize Have students use their completed graphic organizers to summarize the lesson. Then have them compare their summaries to the lesson summary on page 245.

Review and Respond Work through the Review questions with students. If students need additional help comparing and contrasting, use Focus Skill Transparency 4.

Make a Table Have students work with partners. Suggest that they choose heads for the columns on their tables, such as Leader, Branch, Office, How Leader Is Chosen, and Duties to help them gather and organize the information they need. Then they can locate and jot down the information. Students may find it helpful to use a computer to construct their tables.

Leveled Readers Use the Leveled Readers and Procedure Card 5 to build fluency and comprehension.

DIRECTIONS Read aloud the words in Part A. Practice reading aloud the phrases and the sentences in Part B.

Part A

Vocabulary Words		Additional Words	
legislative branch	veto	article	official
bill	appoint	yearly	
executive branch	judicial branch	approve	
budget	appeal	court	

Part B

1. The first article / of the Indiana Constitution / is the Bill of Rights.

2. Indiana's legislative branch / writes state laws.

3. The executive branch / makes sure that state laws / are carried out.

4. One job of the governor / is to create the yearly state budget.

5. The governor / can either approve / or veto / bills the legislature passes.

6. The governor / can appoint people / to lead various departments, / such as the Department of Agriculture.

7. The judicial branch / is made up of all the state's judges / and courts.

8. A person not satisfied / with the result of a trial / can appeal, / or ask that it be judged again / in a higher court.

9. The governor / is the top official / in the state.

10. Indiana's state government / is made up of many officials / working together.

YOU ARE THERE Turn to Student Edition page 240. Practice reading aloud "You Are There" three times. Try to improve your reading each time. Record your best time on the line below.

Number of words ____74____ My Best Time _____ Words per Minute _____

Name _____ Date _____

Lesson Title: _____

Indiana's Constitution

Purposes _____ .

Bill of Rights What it outlines _____

Branches of Government

Where leaders have offices _____

The Legislative Branch

What it does _____
_____

Called _____

Houses _____
_____

The Executive Branch

What it does _____
_____

Leader _____

Has many _____

The Judicial Branch

What it does _____
_____
_____
_____

Highest court _____
_____

State Leaders

State Offices

Top official in state _____

Second-highest _____

Third-highest _____

Top judge _____

The Federal System

Who shares power _____
_____

What Indiana voters do _____
_____
_____

LESSON 5 Indiana's Local Governments

Vocabulary Strategies

Preteach Additional Vocabulary After teaching the Vocabulary words on Student Edition page 246, explain to students that there are several other important words they will see in this lesson. Use Procedure Card 1, along with the suggestions below, to introduce the words.

county	Ask students to name the county they live in. On a map, point out your county and nearby counties.
trustee	Point out the base word *trust* and suffix *-ee*. Remind students that the suffix *-ee* often refers to a person, as in *employee*. A trustee is a person who is given a position of trust or leadership.
board	Have students give meanings they know for this word. Explain that a board can be a group of people who make decisions, such as a board of education.
unique	Tell students that this word is from the Latin *unus*, meaning "one." Something that is unique is the only one of its kind. Other words from this root include *unit, unite, union, unity*.
overlap	Use two sheets of paper to demonstrate the meaning of *overlap*. Then discuss how duties or responsibilities might overlap.
tax	Invite students to share information about taxes. Explain that governments collect money from citizens to help support the government and to pay for the goods and services it provides.

WORD CARDS To help teach the lesson vocabulary, use the Word Cards on pages 147–150.

Build Fluency

Use page 96 and the steps on Procedure Card 2 to reinforce vocabulary and build fluency. Read each vocabulary word aloud and have students repeat it. Then have students work in pairs to reread the words. Follow a similar procedure with the phrases and sentences. Continue to help students build fluency by having them reread "You Are There" in the Student Edition.

BEFORE READING

Preview the Lesson Guide students in previewing the lesson using Procedure Card 3. Point out the following features of the lesson on Student Edition pages 246–249.

• **Pages 246–247** Read aloud the "What to Know" question. Preview the photograph of the Fulton County Courthouse on page 246. Ask if students know where the county courthouse of their county is located. Preview the photograph on page 247 and tell briefly what Unigov is and how it is different from other city and county governments. Then ask what students have learned so far about local governments of Indiana from these photographs and captions.

• **Pages 248–249** Preview the photographs showing different services that local governments provide. Invite students to tell why each of these services is important to the taxpayers who help pay for them. Preview the Review questions on page 249.

DURING READING

Build Comprehension of Expository Text Present the graphic organizer on page 97. Have students preview the organizer by filling in the lesson title and comparing the two main heads in the organizer with the matching subheads in the Student Edition pages 246–249. Tell students that the section subheads provide additional help with identifying important information. Use Procedure Card 4, the Reading Check questions in *Indiana Social Studies*, and the directed reading suggestions below.

• **Page 246** After students have read "You Are There," have them recall the name of the city where their own county courthouse is located. If possible, show students a picture of their county courthouse.

• **Page 247** After students have read "Local Governments," have them identify their own county, county seat, township, city or town, and school district. Briefly discuss how your local governments are led, and mention any names of government leaders that students may recognize. Then have students fill in the first part of the graphic organizer. Point out that the subhead in the box matches the section subhead in the text.

• **Pages 248–249** Have students read "Government Services" and complete the remaining two boxes in the organizer. Tell students to list under "Providing Services" all the different types of governments they read about that provide services for citizens.

AFTER READING

Summarize Have students use their completed graphic organizers to summarize the lesson. Then have them compare their summaries to the lesson summary on page 249.

Review and Respond Work through the Review questions with students. If students need additional help comparing and contrasting, use Focus Skill Transparency 4.

Write a List Students might use local government web sites and publications to find information about services these governments provide. Extend the activity by having small groups of students meet to combine their individual lists into a master list. Then have each group create an illustrated pamphlet to share information about the services their local governments provide.

Leveled Readers Use the Leveled Readers and Procedure Card 5 to build fluency and comprehension.

Name _____ Date _____

DIRECTIONS   Read aloud the words in Part A. Practice reading aloud the
phrases and the sentences in Part B.

Part A

Vocabulary Words	Additional Words	
county seat	county	unique
municipal	trustee	overlap
income	board	tax

Part B

1. Indiana / is divided / into 92 counties.

2. Most county governments / meet at county courthouses / or nearby
   offices.

3. The city in which the county courthouse is located / is the county seat.

4. Each township in a county / is led by a township trustee / and board.

5. The governments of cities and towns / are called municipal governments.

6. Indianapolis and Marion County / have a unique government / called
   Unigov.

7. Special districts, / which usually provide / one service, / overlap with
   county / and city governments.

8. To pay / for the goods and services they provide, / the state and local
   governments / collect taxes.

9. Governments / tax people's income.

YOU ARE THERE Turn to Student Edition page 246. Practice reading aloud "You Are There"
three times. Try to improve your reading each time. Record your best time on
the line below.

Number of words ___62___ My Best Time _____ Words per Minute _____

Lesson Title: _____

Local Governments

From Counties to Districts

How many counties _____ Most led by _____

_____

Counties divided into _____ Led by _____

Cities and towns usually led by _____

City legislature _____ Town legislature _____

Where special districts are found _____

Why special districts are set up _____

Government Services

Providing Services

Governments that provide services

_____

_____

_____

_____

Paying for Government

How _____

Types of taxes _____

_____

_____

_____

LESSON 6 Indiana Citizenship

Vocabulary Strategies

Preteach Additional Vocabulary After teaching the Vocabulary words on Student Edition page 252, explain to students that there are several other important words they will see in this lesson. Use Procedure Card 1, along with the suggestions below, to introduce the words.

guarantee	Ask whether students have ever heard products advertised with a money-back guarantee. Explain that to guarantee something means to promise or make sure that it happens.
informed	Write *inform*, *informed*, and *information*. Tell students that an informed citizen is someone who has knowledge or information about issues and problems. Ask how citizens can become informed.
candidate	Tell students that a candidate is someone who is trying to get elected to public office. For example, candidates may be trying to get elected to the office of President, governor, or mayor.
trait	Have students list some traits, or qualities, that they think good citizens should have.
common	Point out that this word has more than one meaning. Discuss its meaning in this context: "Another responsibility involved in being a good citizen is working for the common good."

WORD CARDS To help teach the lesson vocabulary, use the Word Cards on pages 149–150.

Build Fluency

Use page 96 and the steps on Procedure Card 2 to reinforce vocabulary and build fluency. Read each vocabulary word aloud and have students repeat it. Then have students work in pairs to reread the words. Follow a similar procedure with the phrases and sentences. Continue to help students build fluency by having them reread "You Are There" in the Student Edition.

BEFORE READING

Preview the Lesson Guide students in previewing the lesson using Procedure Card 3. Point out the following features of the lesson on Student Edition pages 252–257.

- **Pages 252–253** Read aloud the "What to Know" question. Preview the photograph of students visiting the Indiana Supreme Court on Constitution Day and Citizenship Day. Have students read and discuss the Fast Fact.

- **Pages 254–255** Preview the photographs on page 254. Discuss what each of these photographs shows about being a good citizen. Have students read the Children in History feature on Ryan White and discuss the Make It Relevant question.

- **Pages 256–257** Preview the photograph of Raven Peterson receiving a national award. Tell students that they will read in the lesson about the volunteer work that Raven did. Preview the Review questions. Then call attention to the biography of community leader and volunteer Yvonne Shaheen on page 257.

DURING READING

Build Comprehension of Expository Text Present the graphic organizer on page 101. Have students preview the organizer by filling in the lesson title and comparing the three main heads in the organizer with the matching subheads in the Student Edition pages 252–256. Tell students that the section subheads provide additional help with identifying important information. Use Procedure Card 4, the Reading Check questions in *Indiana Social Studies*, and the directed reading suggestions below.

- **Page 252** After students have read "You Are There," ask whether they think it is important to celebrate events like Constitution Day and Citizenship Day, and why or why not. Encourage students to offer ideas for other ways to celebrate this special holiday.

- **Page 253** Have students read "Hoosier Rights and Responsibilities" and fill in the first box in the graphic organizer. Point out the placement of the subhead "Citizen Responsibilities" that matches the section subhead in the text.

- **Page 254** After students have read "Taking Part," discuss ways that people can help make their community and country a better place. Then have students fill in the next box of the organizer. Remind them to use the three subheads to help them locate information in the text.

- **Pages 255–256** Have students read and discuss "Civic Virtues." Then they can use the four subheads to help them complete the organizer.

AFTER READING

Summarize Have students use their completed graphic organizers to summarize the lesson. Then have them compare their summaries to the lesson summary on page 256.

Review and Respond Work through the Review questions with students. If students need additional help comparing and contrasting, use Focus Skill Transparency 4.

Write a Newspaper Article Have students brainstorm issues they might write about. Alternatively, you may want to identify some issues that have been in the news recently. After listing several issues, discuss how students might go about researching them. You may want to suggest articles and websites that are relevant to specific issues. Remind students that newspaper articles tell When, Where, Who, What, and Why.

Leveled Readers Use the Leveled Readers and Procedure Card 5 to build fluency and comprehension.

Name _____ Date _____

DIRECTIONS   Read aloud the words in Part A. Practice reading aloud the phrases and the sentences in Part B.

Part A

Vocabulary Words		Additional Words	
register	civic virtue	guarantee	trait
citizenship	civility	informed	common
public service		candidate	

Part B

1. Hoosiers / have many rights / guaranteed by the Indiana Constitution.

2. In Indiana, / a citizen 18 years old or older / must register to vote / before an election.

3. With voting / comes the responsibility / of being an informed citizen.

4. Voters / should prepare / by learning about important issues / and about the candidates.

5. All citizens of Indiana / and the United States / enjoy the rights of citizenship.

6. Being a government leader / is one kind of public service.

7. Communities in Indiana / depend on their citizens / to show certain civic virtues.

8. Civility / is an important trait / needed to work with others / in a community.

9. Another responsibility / involved in being a good citizen / is working for the common good.

YOU ARE THERE   Turn to Student Edition page 252. Practice reading aloud "You Are There" three times. Try to improve your reading each time. Record your best time on the line below.

Number of words ___92___   My Best Time _____   Words per Minute _____

Name _____ Date _____

Lesson Title: _____

Hoosier Rights and Responsibilities

Rights include _____

Citizen Responsibilities

Stated in laws _____

Not required by law _____

Taking Part

Volunteering How _____

Public Service How _____

Patriotism How _____

Civic Virtues

Respect for Others Important trait _____

Individual Responsibility What good citizens do _____
_____

The Common Good Example _____

Demonstrating Civic Virtues When _____ Where _____
_____

Teacher Notes

_____

_____

_____

_____

_____

_____

_____

_____

_____

_____

_____

_____

_____

_____

_____

_____

Use the following steps to introduce the Additional Words in each lesson.

1. Write the word on the board or on chart paper.

2. Say the word aloud.

3. Track the word and have students repeat it.

4. Give the meaning of the word or context that makes the meaning clear. For example, you might

   ● demonstrate or dramatize the meaning

   ● point out meanings of roots, root words, prefixes, and suffixes

   ● point out endings such as *-ed* and *-ing*

   ● give examples

   ● give synonyms or antonyms

   ● relate to familiar concepts

   ● draw a sketch or display a picture

Suggested Vocabulary Activities Use or adapt the following activities to give students further practice using Vocabulary Words and Additional Words.

FRAYER MODEL

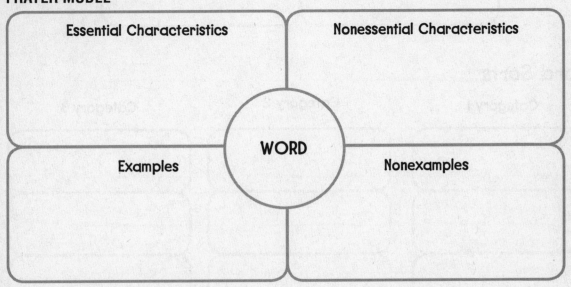

(continued)

Semantic Mapping

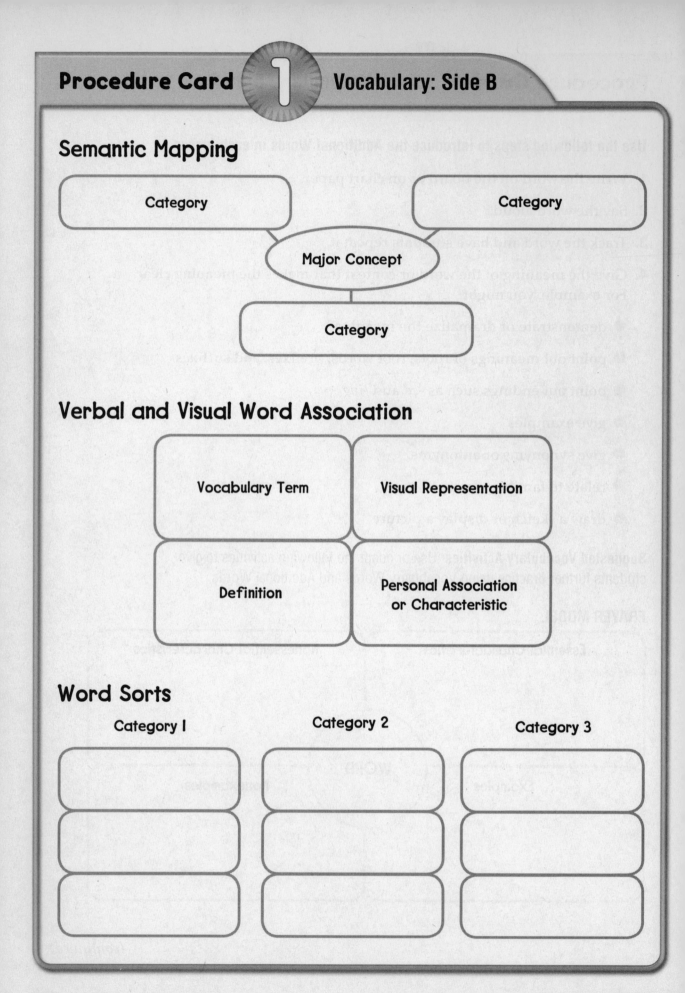

Category	Category

Major Concept

Category

Verbal and Visual Word Association

Vocabulary Term	Visual Representation
Definition	Personal Association or Characteristic

Word Sorts

Category 1	Category 2	Category 3

Use the following steps to help students build fluency.

Vocabulary Words

1. Read each vocabulary word aloud and have students repeat it.

2. Then have students work in pairs to read the vocabulary words aloud to each other.

3. Follow the same procedure with the additional words.

4. After partners have practiced reading aloud the words in each list by themselves, have them listen to each other as they practice the entire list.

Sentences

1. Read each sentence aloud and have students repeat it. As you read, model natural phrasing (intonation and rhythm), pacing, and tone.

2. Then read the sentences aloud as a coherent text. Point out that the sentences read together give a preview of the content of the lesson.

3. Have students practice reading the phrases and sentences with a partner. When the partners are satisfied with their progress, have them practice reading the sentences as a text several times.

(continued)

Help students continue to build fluency by having them do oral rereadings of "You Are There" in the Student Edition. Provide them with a stopwatch to time themselves on each reading.

Choose from the following options for the repeated readings.

- Students read the passage aloud to their partners three times. The reader rates his or her own reading on a scale of 1–4. The partner offers positive comments on the reader's improvement.

- Students read the passage aloud to themselves three times and rate their own reading on a scale of 1–4. Encourage students to note ways in which they have improved from one reading to the next.

- Students read the passage aloud into a tape recorder three times. After they listen to each reading, they rate the reading on a scale of 1–4. Then they listen to previous readings and compare to note improvements.

Use the following steps to preview the lesson with students.

1. Read aloud the title of the lesson.

2. Have students look over each page. Call attention to text features such as the following:

   ● the "What to Know" question

   ● time lines

   ● subheads

   ● illustrations and captions

   ● maps, charts, graphs, and other visual aids

   ● features such as Primary Sources and Children in History

   ● words that are highlighted in the text

   ● Review questions

3. Discuss each text feature as needed to help students understand how it relates to the topic of the lesson.

4. Work with students to set a purpose for reading the first section of the lesson by turning the first subhead into a question. Remind them to use this strategy as they read each section of the lesson.

Choose from the following options to have students read the text and complete the graphic organizer.

Reading the Text

- Have students read the lesson silently to themselves.

- Have students read together in pairs. Where possible, pair a struggling reader with a more proficient reader. Partners may take turns reading sections of the lesson aloud to each other.

- Have students read in pairs. Partners read together silently, pausing often to discuss and summarize what they have read so far.

- Have students take turns reading sections of the lesson aloud to the group.

Completing the Graphic Organizer

- If students are reading in pairs, they may work with their partners to complete the graphic organizer.

- If students are not reading in pairs, you may want to assign partners for the purpose of completing the graphic organizer.

Leveled Readers

Before Reading

1. Build background by talking about the topic of the book.

2. Discuss the cover illustration. Have children track the print as you read the title and the name of the author.

3. Preview the book by discussing the first few illustrations. Ask children what they think the book is about.

4. Help children set a purpose for reading.

During Reading

1. Have children read one or two pages at a time. If necessary, read the pages aloud as children follow along.

2. Ask questions about each page or set of pages to check children's comprehension.

3. Define any unfamiliar words, using illustrations, gestures, or context sentences.

4. Occasionally ask children to summarize or retell what they have read so far.

After Reading

1. Discuss what children liked about the book. Then guide them to summarize or retell the selection.

2. Have children respond to the book through discussion, drama, art, writing, or another appropriate activity.

You can use a KWL chart to guide your reading. Follow the steps.

Step 1. Before you read the lesson, make a KWL chart like this one.

K What we know	W What we want to find out	L What we learned

Step 2. Read the title of the lesson. Discuss with your partner or group what you already know about the topic of this lesson. For instance, you may have information from previous social studies chapters or from other sources.

Step 3. Record the information you already know in the K column of the chart. Keep in mind that sometimes information that we think we know may turn out to be incorrect. As you read the lesson, look back at the K column to check whether each fact you listed is correct.

Step 4. Preview the lesson by reading the subheads and looking at time lines, maps, illustrations, and other special features. Discuss what you want to find out when you read the lesson. One way to do this is by asking questions about the subheads. Record your questions in the W column of the chart.

Step 5. Read the lesson. As you find information to answer your questions, record the answers in the L column of the chart.

Step 6. Use your completed KWL chart to review and summarize the lesson.

You can use the SQ3R strategy to guide your reading. The letters SQRRR stand for the steps in the process—Survey, Question, Read, Recite, and Review.

Step 1. SURVEY

- Read the title of the lesson. Ask yourself what you know about the topic and what you want to find out about it.
- Read the lesson subheads and skim the first sentences of sections or paragraphs.
- Look over illustrations, maps, graphic aids, and special features.
- Read the first paragraph of the lesson.
- Read the lesson summary.

Step 2. QUESTION

- Set your main purpose for reading by turning the title of the lesson into a question.
- Write down questions you thought of during your survey.
- Set a purpose for reading each section of the lesson by turning each subhead into a question.
- Ask yourself questions about illustrations, graphic aids, and special features.
- Write down unfamiliar words and find out what they mean.

Step 3. READ

- Read to find answers to your questions.
- Use the answers to your questions to be sure you understand each section of the lesson.
- If there are ideas or words that you don't understand, ask yourself more questions.

(continued)

Step 4. RECITE

- Look away from the book and your questions to recall what you have read.
- Recite the answers to your questions aloud or write them down.
- Reread the lesson to find answers to questions that you have not already answered.

Step 5. REVIEW

- Answer the main purpose question that you formed from the lesson title.
- Look over the answers to the questions formed from the subheads and any other questions you had.
- Summarize the lesson by creating a graphic organizer, discussing the lesson with your partner or group, or writing a summary.

Student Card 3 QAR Strategy

What is QAR? The letters QAR stand for Question-Answer Relationship. You can use the QAR strategy to help you answer questions as you read and the Review questions at the end of each lesson.

Step 1. Read the information in the chart to learn about the four types of questions.

Question-Answer Relationships (QAR)

in the text

"Right There"	"Think and Search"
The answer is stated in a single sentence in the text.	The answer is not stated directly but can be found in several sentences or parts of the text.

based on what you already know

"Author and You"	"On My Own"
You need to read the text to understand the question, but the answer is not found in the text.	You can answer the question based on what you already know without reading the text.

Step 2. Before you answer a question, identify which type of question it is. Decide what you will need to do in order to answer the question.

Step 3. Use the text, what you already know, or both to answer the question.

Build Fluency Words per Minute Formula

Use the following formula to calculate words per minute:

1. Count the words in the passage.

2. Record the student's reading time in seconds.

3. Divide the number of words by the number of seconds.

4. Multiply (number of words per second) by 60 to convert to words per minute.

Here is an example:

1. 90 words (in the passage)

2. 75 seconds (student's reading time)

3. $90 \div 75 = 1.2$ (words per second)

4. $1.2 \times 60 = 72$ words per minute

Answer Key

Lesson 1 The Geography of Indiana, p. 5

Indiana in the United States
the Midwest; four

Indiana's Land and Water
wide plains, fertile soils, farming; more variety, plains and hills; the Wabash River; in northern Indiana

Indiana's Cities
Indianapolis; in the center of the state; Muncie, Lafayette, Kokomo, Anderson; Fort Wayne, South Bend, Gary, Hammond; Evansville, Bloomington, New Albany

Lesson 2 Physical Regions of Indiana, p. 9

Rivers of Ice
glaciers; flattened much of state, formed many rivers and lakes

Northern Moraine and Lake
northern one-third of Indiana; natural lakes and moraines; wetlands; along Lake Michigan

Central Till Plain
South of the Northern Moraine and Lake region; its best farmland

Southern Hills and Lowlands
the southern one-third of Indiana; strip of lowland followed by strip of upland; Weed Patch Hill

Lesson 3 Climate and Wildlife of Indiana, p. 13

Indiana's Climate
temperate; precipitation

Earth and Sun
It is summer there; It is winter there.

Precipitation
Lake Michigan; 40 inches each year

Indiana's Wildlife
yellow poplar; Examples may vary; cardinal; Examples may vary.

Lesson 4 People and Resources of Indiana, p. 17

Indiana's Resources
fertile soil and flat land; coal, oil, natural gas, minerals, limestone, forests

Modifying the Land
cleared forests, drained wetlands; built roads, canals, and railroads; mined and drilled for fuels, built dams, replanted forests; cleared forests to build towns, towns grew into cities

Urban Challenges
traffic jams and air pollution; more demand for services

Lesson 5 People of Indiana, p. 21

Indiana's Population
about 170 people per square mile; in cities and suburbs

Where Hoosiers Come From
grown and changed; Native Americans; settlers, immigrants, African Americans; Hispanics, Asians; in the state; at festivals, museums, state parks

Religion in Indiana
Roman Catholic priests; Protestant beliefs; Roman Catholics, Protestants, Jewish, Muslims, Buddhists, Hindus

Lesson 6 Famous Hoosiers, p. 25

Sports
Indiana Pacers, Indiana University Hoosiers, Notre Dame Fighting Irish; Answers may vary but should include information about the Indy 500 and other sports mentioned in the text.

Literature and Art
Answers may vary but should include names and correct information about writers, poets, and artists mentioned in the text.

Music
Answers may vary but should include names and correct information about musicians, festivals, and concerts mentioned in the text, and about Twyla Tharp.

Broadway and Hollywood
Answers may vary but should include names and correct information about entertainment figures mentioned in the text.

Lesson 1 Early People of Indiana, p. 29

Long, Long Ago
Paleo-Indians; more than 12,000 years ago

New Ways of Life
warmer climate caused larger animals to become extinct; Archaic Indians; smaller animals, plants, nuts, berries, mussels; about 3,000 years ago; began to farm, built permanent shelters, formed villages, used boats to trade

Building Mounds
about 3,000 years ago; Woodland Indians; built mounds for many purposes; about 1,000 years ago; the Mississippian people; 11

Lesson 2 Native Peoples of Indiana, p. 33

Tribes and Culture
by 1650; Its ways of living made up a tribe's culture; Depending on where they lived, tribes used different natural resources.

The Miami
many settlements, elected chiefs, lived in wigwams, hunted and farmed

The Shawnee
used canoes for travel and trade, hunted small animals; families had different responsibilities

The Lenape
in the 1770s; wigwams and longhouses, farmed, hunted, fished, traded

The Potawatomi
They used the resources around them to meet their needs. Every person belonged to a clan.

Learning from the Past
We learn about Native Americans from the artifacts they left behind. We learn about Native American ways of life from stories, songs, and teachings.

Lesson 3 Exploration and Settlement, p. 37

Exploring the Americas
1492; Christopher Columbus; claimed vast areas of land in North America and South America

Exploring Indiana
Sieur de La Salle; 1679

The Fur Trade
fur traders; missionaries; in Europe; goods such as tools, knives, guns, blankets, and beads; changed the way they lived

War over Land
Vincennes; 1732; on the Wabash River; 1754; 1763; control of Canada and the French lands east of the Mississippi River

Lesson 4 The American Revolution, p. 41

A War for Freedom
British government taxed paper goods and other items; that they should not have to follow these laws; because they did have representation in the British government; independence; 1775

The War in Indiana
because they thought the Americans would take their lands; George Rogers Clark; stop attacks by Native Americans and weaken British influence in the West; captured British forts; Clark led a surprise mid-winter attack, recaptured Fort Sackville

The War Ends
1781; General George Washington defeated Lord Cornwallis at Yorktown, Virginia; the Americans

Lesson 5 The Northwest Territory, p. 45

Expanding West
1783; the United States of America; north of the Ohio River

Settling the Northwest Territory
the Land Ordinance of 1785; told how land in the territory would be divided and sold; 1787; a plan for governing the Northwest Territory; Native Americans were unhappy about increasing number of settlers; Native Americans gave up most of their land; 1800; William Henry Harrison; Vincennes; the United States and Britain; 1814

Lesson 6 A New State, p. 49

Steps Toward Statehood
1. Jennings asked Congress to pass an enabling act. 2. President James Madison signed the enabling act into law. 3. Forty-three delegates met in Corydon. 4. A majority voted to apply for statehood. 5. The delegates wrote a constitution.

The Nineteenth State
June 29, 1816; December 11, 1816; the first state government; the basic rights of the people; Jonathan Jennings; Corydon; that the constitution needed to be revised; the Indiana Constitution of 1851

Lesson 1 New Communities, p. 53

A Thriving State
because Indiana had a great deal of land for sale; settlers from other states, Quakers, European immigrants

Growing Communities
a planned community; to help organize local governments; in the center of the state

Transportation
Robert Fulton; early 1800s; by giving farmers a better way to get goods to market; caused the state to take on debt to pay for them; connected towns and states; made travel faster and more dependable

Indian Removal
to make more land available for settlers; Potawatomi and Miami were forced to leave Indiana

Lesson 2 The Civil War, p. 57

North and South
slave states; free states; divided it

Indiana Abolitionists
a system of secret routes ; Chapman Harris, George Baptiste; Levi and Catharine Coffin; to oppose slavery; the Republic of Liberia

The Civil War in Indiana
1861; about 200,000; the Battle of Corydon; took over businesses and farms, worked as nurses, worked at the state arsenal; 1863; Abraham Lincoln; Emancipation Proclamation; 1865

Lesson 3 Changes in Indiana, p. 61

Time of Reconstruction
Thirteenth Amendment ended slavery, Fifteenth Amendment says that no citizen can be denied the right to vote because of race; sharecropping; Freedman's Bureau provided food, money, and schools; still faced threats

Industries Grow
new technologies, new farming methods; used natural resources to make products, others started by inventors; government leaders offered free natural gas to industries, glass industry, oil refineries, steel

Changes in Society
formed to improve working conditions; cities grew in late 1800s, city governments faced new

challenges; many schools built, Indiana University founded, private colleges

Lesson 4 A New Century, p. 65

World War I
1914; 1917; about 130,000; farmers, women, people who bought bonds

The Great Migration
between 1910 and 1930; thousands of African Americans moved North; unfairly; started businesses, published newspapers, took charge of schools

Women Gain the Vote
woman's suffrage and other rights; August 26, 1920

Developments in Indiana
automobile and interurban rail; making consumer goods; mechanization

Lesson 5 Challenging Times, p. 69

The Great Depression
1920s; fast growth, people borrowed money to buy stocks; October 1929; helped lead to the Great Depression, banks closed, people lost savings

The Government Helps
cut back production or closed; 1932; Franklin D. Roosevelt; the New Deal; set up programs to give people jobs

World War II
1939; December 7, 1941; produced war equipment and food; rationing, planted victory gardens, recycled; 1945

Lesson 6 Into Modern Times, p. 73

Growth After World War II
population grew; good jobs; new highways, houses in suburbs, ports

The Korean War
Cold War; North Korean soldiers invaded South Korea; many soldiers from Indiana fought, ended in 1953

The Vietnam War
War between North and South Vietnam, United States sent many soldiers; Some supported the war, others protested.

Civil Rights
equal housing, education, jobs for all; Civil Rights Act of 1964; African Americans in Indiana gained more power in government

Immigration
population grew and changed, immigrants came from all over the world, helped businesses grow,

have started many businesses, contributed to the state's culture

Lesson 7 Recent Times, p. 77

Facing New Dangers
terrorism; On September 11, 2001, terrorists flew airplanes into buildings in the United States. President Bush called for a War on Terrorism. He set up the Department of Homeland Security.

Businesses Change
Farming companies built large farms. New equipment helped farmers raise more crops using fewer workers. Some factories shut down in the 1960s. New machines cut costs and put many Indiana steelworkers out of work. New technology helped some Indiana factories succeed. Service industries grew rapidly in the 1980s and 1990s.

High Technology in Indiana
Companies in Indiana make medical products, CDs, and other products. About 100 aerospace companies are located in Indiana. More than 20 astronauts were educated at Purdue.

Lesson 1 Indiana Industries, p. 81

Indiana's Economy
diverse; about $215 billion; has increased dramatically

A Changing Economy
agriculture; manufacturing and services; merchants and banks; more workers with education; new technologies

The Economy Today
more diverse; by machines; nearly one-fourth of state's workers; nearly two-thirds of state's workers; grown in Indiana

Lesson 2 Indiana's Entrepreneurs, p. 85

Entrepreneurs
because they hope to make a profit

Early Entrepreneurs
Eli Lilly; Eli Lilly and Company, pharmaceutical company; Ball brothers; Ball Corporation, products from food containers to space equipment; Studebaker brothers; Studebaker Corporation, began building wagons, then built cars; Madame C. J. Walker; cosmetic and hair products for African American women; Marie

Webster; quilt patterns; Clessie Lyle Cummins; Cummins Engine Company, diesel engines; Orville Redenbacher; popcorn

Entrepreneurs Today
more than 430,000; help it grow

Lesson 3 Trade in Indiana, p. 89

Supply and Demand
increase; decrease

Trading Within Indiana
along the Great Lakes and on Indiana's rivers; by land, water, and air

Trading with Other States
Illinois, Wisconsin, Ohio, Michigan; resources, products, and services

Trading with the World
resources, products, and services; about 200

Lesson 4 Indiana's State Government, p. 93

Indiana's Constitution
to establish justice, keep public order, and make sure freedom lasts; the rights and freedoms of Indiana citizens

Branches of Government
Indiana's Statehouse; writes state laws; the General Assembly; Senate, House of Representatives; makes sure that state laws are carried out; governor; duties and powers; decides whether laws agree with constitution, makes sure laws are carried out fairly; Indiana Supreme Court

State Leaders
governor; lieutenant governor; secretary of state; chief justice of supreme court

The Federal System
national and state governments; elect leaders to represent them in the United States Congress

Lesson 5 Indiana's Local Governments, p. 97

Local Governments
92; three county commissioners and a county council; townships; a township trustee and board; elected mayors; city council; town council; throughout the state; to handle a single issue

Government Services
state government, county governments, townships, cities and towns, special districts; by collecting taxes; income tax, sales tax, property tax, taxes on vehicles and gasoline

Lesson 6 Indiana Citizenship, p. 101

Hoosier Rights and Responsibilities
the right to vote, the right to hold office; pay
taxes, obey laws, serve on juries; voting, being an
informed citizen

Taking Part
helping others in their communities; being a
government leader, being an active citizen;
displaying the flag, reciting the Pledge of
Allegiance

Civic Virtues
civility; show self-discipline, obey laws, are
honest and fair, stand up for what they believe in;
helping clean up a community park OR helping
the homeless; every day; in school, at home, and
in the community

region Unit 1, Lesson 1	**tributary** Unit 1, Lesson 1
relative location Unit 1, Lesson 1	**human feature** Unit 1, Lesson 1
border Unit 1, Lesson 1	**industry** Unit 1, Lesson 1
physical feature Unit 1, Lesson 1	**glacier** Unit 1, Lesson 2
plain Unit 1, Lesson 1	**lithosphere** Unit 1, Lesson 2
fertile soil Unit 1, Lesson 1	**wetland** Unit 1, Lesson 2

A stream or river that flows into a larger stream or river.	An area with at least one feature that makes it different from other areas.
Something created by people that alters the landscape.	Where a place is in relation to other places on Earth.
All the businesses that make one kind of product or do one kind of service.	A line that divides one place from another.
A huge, slow-moving mass of ice.	Climate, water, or landforms.
The soil and rock that form Earth's surface.	An area of low, flat land.
Low-lying land where the water level is always near or above the surface of the land.	Soil good for growing crops.

dune Unit 1, Lesson 2	**tornado** Unit 1, Lesson 3
till Unit 1, Lesson 2	**precipitation** Unit 1, Lesson 3
elevation Unit 1, Lesson 2	**drought** Unit 1, Lesson 3
canyon Unit 1, Lesson 2	**hydrosphere** Unit 1, Lesson 3
sinkhole Unit 1, Lesson 2	**biosphere** Unit 1, Lesson 3
climate Unit 1, Lesson 3	**natural resource** Unit 1, Lesson 4

A funnel-shaped, spinning windstorm.	A hill of sand built up by wind.
Water that falls to Earth's surface as rain, sleet, hail, or snow.	A mixture of clay, sand, and small stones that makes soil very rich.
A long period of little or no precipitation.	The height of land above or below sea level.
The system of water below, on, and above Earth's surface.	A deep, narrow valley with steep sides.
All the living things and their environment.	A large, bowl-shaped hole that forms when limestone layers above an underground hole collapse.
Something found in nature that people can use.	The kind of weather a place has over a long period of time.

agriculture	culture
Unit 1, Lesson 4	Unit 1, Lesson 5
mineral	**population density**
Unit 1, Lesson 4	Unit 1, Lesson 5
canal	**population distribution**
Unit 1, Lesson 4	Unit 1, Lesson 5
rural	**immigrant**
Unit 1, Lesson 4	Unit 1, Lesson 5
urban	**heritage**
Unit 1, Lesson 4	Unit 1, Lesson 5
suburb	**ethnic group**
Unit 1, Lesson 4	Unit 1, Lesson 5

A way of life shared by a group of people.	The growing of crops and the raising of farm animals.
The number of people who live in an area of a certain size.	A natural nonliving substance.
The way in which a population is spread out over an area.	A human-made waterway that connects two bodies of water.
A person who comes from one country to live in another country.	Like, in, or of the country.
Ways of life, including customs and traditions, that are passed down through families.	Like, in, or of a city.
A group of people from the same country, of the same race, or with a shared culture.	A smaller community near a city.

dialect

Unit 1, Lesson 6

science fiction

Unit 1, Lesson 6

pop art

Unit 1, Lesson 6

choreographer

Unit 1, Lesson 6

	A way of speaking.
	Fiction that deals with the influence on society of real or imagined science.
	An art style that uses common objects.
	A person who creates dances.

nomad Unit 2, Lesson 1	**historic** Unit 2, Lesson 2
ancestor Unit 2, Lesson 1	**tribe** Unit 2, Lesson 2
extinct Unit 2, Lesson 1	**specialize** Unit 2, Lesson 2
mound Unit 2, Lesson 1	**longhouse** Unit 2, Lesson 2
permanent Unit 2, Lesson 1	**clan** Unit 2, Lesson 2
barter Unit 2, Lesson 1	**artifact** Unit 2, Lesson 2

Something or someone who lived after written history.	A person who has no permanent home and moves from place to place.
A group that shares the same language and has the same leaders.	An early family member.
To work at one kind of job and learn to do it well.	No longer in existence, which is what happens to a living thing when all of its kind die out.
A large rectangular building made from wooden poles and bark in which several families could live.	A large pile of hard-packed earth and other materials.
A group of closely related people.	Long-lasting.
A object made by people in the past.	To trade goods, usually without using money.

legend	voyageur
Unit 2, Lesson 2	Unit 2, Lesson 3
explorer	allies
Unit 2, Lesson 3	Unit 2, Lesson 3
colony	treaty
Unit 2, Lesson 3	Unit 2, Lesson 3
expedition	proclamation
Unit 2, Lesson 3	Unit 2, Lesson 3
missionary	tax
Unit 2, Lesson 3	Unit 2, Lesson 4
scarce	independence
Unit 2, Lesson 3	Unit 2, Lesson 4

A French word meaning "traveler."	A story handed down over time.
Partners in war.	Someone who travels to unfamiliar places.
An agreement among nations or groups.	A settlement that is ruled by a faraway government.
A public announcement.	A journey into an area to learn more about it.
Money a government collects from citizens for the services it provides.	A person who teaches his or her religious beliefs to others.
The freedom to govern on one's own.	Hard to find.

revolution Unit 2, Lesson 4	**township** Unit 2, Lesson 5
militia Unit 2, Lesson 4	**right** Unit 2, Lesson 5
surrender Unit 2, Lesson 4	**census** Unit 2, Lesson 6
debt Unit 2, Lesson 5	**enabling act** Unit 2, Lesson 6
territory Unit 2, Lesson 5	**delegate** Unit 2, Lesson 6
ordinance Unit 2, Lesson 5	**constitution** Unit 2, Lesson 6

One of the squares of land that the Northwest Territory was divided into by the Land Ordinance of 1785.	A sudden, complete change of government.
A freedom that belongs to a person.	A volunteer army.
Official population count.	To give up.
A special law that allowed a territory to become a state.	Something owed to someone else, often money.
A representative.	An area owned and governed by a country.
A written plan for government.	A law or set of laws.

slavery	
Unit 2, Lesson 6	
illegal	
Unit 2, Lesson 6	

	The practice of holding people against their will and forcing them to work.
	Against the law.

migration Unit 3, Lesson 1	**slave state** Unit 3, Lesson 2
flatboat Unit 3, Lesson 1	**free state** Unit 3, Lesson 2
steamboat Unit 3, Lesson 1	**abolitionist** Unit 3, Lesson 2
navigable Unit 3, Lesson 1	**Underground Railroad** Unit 3, Lesson 2
stagecoach Unit 3, Lesson 1	**secede** Unit 3, Lesson 2
plantation Unit 3, Lesson 2	**civil war** Unit 3, Lesson 2

A state that allowed slavery before the Civil War.	The movement of people from one place to live in another place.
A state where slavery was against the law before the Civil War.	A large, flat-bottomed boat that could only float downstream.
A person who worked to end slavery.	A boat powered by a steam engine that turns a large paddle wheel.
A system of secret escape routes that led enslaved people to free land.	Wide and deep enough for ships to use.
To withdraw from a group, often to form another group.	An enclosed wagon that carried passengers and was pulled by horses.
A war between people in the same country.	A huge farm that grows crops such as cotton, rice, and tobacco.

Reconstruction Unit 3, Lesson 3	**bond** Unit 3, Lesson 4
sharecropping Unit 3, Lesson 3	**suffrage** Unit 3, Lesson 4
automobile Unit 3, Lesson 3	**interurban rail** Unit 3, Lesson 4
manufacturing Unit 3, Lesson 3	**consumer goods** Unit 3, Lesson 4
refinery Unit 3, Lesson 3	**stock** Unit 3, Lesson 5
labor union Unit 3, Lesson 3	**depression** Unit 3, Lesson 5

Document that allows the government to use people's money for a certain amount of time and pay it back later.	A period of rebuilding the nation after the Civil War.
The right to vote.	Farming a landowner's property for a share of the crops.
A network of rail lines connecting rural areas with nearby cities and towns.	A vehicle that can move by itself, powered by its own engine; a car.
Products made for personal use.	The making of goods from raw materials by hand or with machinery.
A share of ownership in a company.	A factory in which resources such as oil are made into products people can use.
A time when there are few jobs and people have little money.	A group of workers who join together to improve their working conditions.

unemployed Unit 3, Lesson 5	**cease-fire** Unit 3, Lesson 6
shortage Unit 3, Lesson 5	**civil rights** Unit 3, Lesson 6
rationing Unit 3, Lesson 5	**discrimination** Unit 3, Lesson 6
recycle Unit 3, Lesson 5	**segregation** Unit 3, Lesson 6
communism Unit 3, Lesson 6	**terrorism** Unit 3, Lesson 7
cold war Unit 3, Lesson 6	**efficient** Unit 3, Lesson 7

A temporary end to a conflict.	Without a job.
The rights of citizens to equal treatment.	A low supply of something.
The unfair treatment of people based on the color of their skin, their religion, or their ethnic group.	The limiting of the amount of what people can buy.
The practice of keeping people from one race or culture separate from other people.	To use again.
The use of violence to promote a cause.	A political and economic system in which all industries, land, and businesses are controlled by the government.
Productive with little waste of time or energy.	A war fought mostly with ideas and money instead of soldiers.

service industry Unit 3, Lesson 7	
high-tech Unit 3, Lesson 7	
aerospace Unit 3, Lesson 7	

	An industry in which workers are paid to do things for other people.
	Shortened form of the words high technology; having to do with inventing, building, or using computers and other kinds of electronic equipment.
	Having to do with the building and testing of equipment for air and space travel.

economy Unit 4, Lesson 1	**tourism** Unit 4, Lesson 1
gross state product Unit 4, Lesson 1	**entrepreneur** Unit 4, Lesson 2
productivity Unit 4, Lesson 1	**profit** Unit 4, Lesson 2
surplus Unit 4, Lesson 1	**investor** Unit 4, Lesson 2
competition Unit 4, Lesson 1	**supply** Unit 4, Lesson 3
ethanol Unit 4, Lesson 1	**demand** Unit 4, Lesson 3

The business of serving visitors.	The way people in a state, region, or country use resources to meet their needs.
A person who takes a risk to start a new business.	The total value of all goods and services produced by workers of a state in a certain year
The money left over after all a business's expenses have been paid.	The amount of goods and services produced in a period of time divided by the resources used to produce them.
A person who puts his or her money at risk in hopes of making a profit.	An amount that is more than what is needed.
The amount of a product or service that is available.	The contest among businesses to sell the most products.
The amount of a product or service that people want and are willing to buy.	A liquid that can be used as a fuel in automobiles.

interdependence Unit 4, Lesson 3	**budget** Unit 4, Lesson 4
export Unit 4, Lesson 3	**veto** Unit 4, Lesson 4
import Unit 4, Lesson 3	**appoint** Unit 4, Lesson 4
legislative branch Unit 4, Lesson 4	**judicial branch** Unit 4, Lesson 4
bill Unit 4, Lesson 4	**appeal** Unit 4, Lesson 4
executive branch Unit 4, Lesson 4	**county seat** Unit 4, Lesson 5

A written plan for how to spend money.	People in each place depend on people in other places for resources, products, and services.
To reject.	A product sent from one country to be sold in another country.
To choose.	A product brought into one country from another country.
The part of government that sees that the laws are carried out fairly.	The part of the government that makes laws.
To ask to have a case judged again in a higher court.	A plan for a new law.
The city or town where the main offices of the county government are located.	The part of government that makes sure laws are carried out.

municipal Unit 4, Lesson 5	**civility** Unit 4, Lesson 6
income Unit 4, Lesson 5	
register Unit 4, Lesson 6	
citizenship Unit 4, Lesson 6	
public service Unit 4, Lesson 6	
civic virtue Unit 4, Lesson 6	

Politeness.	Having to do with a city.
	Money people earn for the work they do.
	To sign up.
	Full membership of a community or country.
	The act of working for the good of a community.
	An action that contributes to the smooth running of a democracy